# INTIMATE TREASON

# Intimate Treason

HEALING THE TRAUMA FOR PARTNERS
CONFRONTING SEX ADDICTION

CLAUDIA BLACK, PhD and
CARA TRIPODI, LCSW

CENTRAL RECOVERY PRESS

CENTRAL RECOVERY PRESS

Central Recovery Press (CRP) is committed to publishing exceptional materials addressing addiction treatment, recovery, and behavioral healthcare topics, including original and quality books, audio/visual communications, and web-based new media. Through a diverse selection of titles, we seek to contribute a broad range of unique resources for professionals, recovering individuals and their families, and the general public.

For more information, visit www.centralrecoverypress.com.

Central Recovery Press, Las Vegas, NV 89129

Publisher:    Central Recovery Press
              3321 N. Buffalo Drive
              Las Vegas, NV 89129

17 16 15 14 13 12    1 2 3 4 5

ISBN-13: 978-1-936290-93-2 (paper)
ISBN-13: 978-1-937612-01-6 (e-book)

Photo of Claudia Black © Brad Reed Photography. Used with permission.
Photo of Cara Tripodi © Sam Fritch Photography. Used with permission.
Image on page 54, used with permission from University of Minnesota Extension Publication #07421; Change: Loss, Opportunity and Resilience by Dr. Sharon M. Danes, Professor, University of Minnesota.

**Publisher's Note:** This book contains general information about sex addiction and its effects on relationships. Central Recovery Press makes no representations or warranties in relation to the information herein; it is not an alternative to medical advice from your doctor or other professional healthcare provider.

Our books represent the experiences and opinions of their authors only. Every effort has been made to ensure that events, institutions, and statistics presented in our books as facts are accurate and up-to-date. To protect their privacy, some of the names of people and institutions have been changed.

*Cover design and interior layout by Sara Streifel, Think Creative Design*

Cara Tripodi dedicates this book to
Kathy Farley—your quiet, steady, and compassionate presence
inspired me personally and professionally. You are greatly missed.


Claudia Black dedicates this book to
Lorie Dwinell—you believed in me and championed me from
the start of my personal recovery and professional growth,
continuing to be by my side all of these years.

# TABLE OF CONTENTS

# ACKNOWLEDGMENTS

**FROM CARA**

To my husband David for his unconditional support and encouragement in the writing of this book. To the many, many partners who taught me how to hear their unique voices and to make meaning about their pain, as well as what they needed to heal. I am forever indebted to you and grateful for the trust you placed in me. To all those who have sought help through STAR and the colleagues over the years whose dedication to healing sex addicts and partners has helped to expand our collective understanding of how to treat this special population. To Martha Turner, MD, for mentoring me; and to Nancy Gambescia, PhD, for her professional acumen over the years.

To Claudia for the chance opportunity to work together. I appreciate the common ground we so easily share in making the voices of partners heard. I am inspired by you and your work and greatly appreciate your tireless dedication to details.

**FROM CLAUDIA**

A special thank you to Diane Dillon; we stepped into the journey many years ago, working with partners and creating a dynamic and inspirational collaboration that has led to the healing of an exponential number of partners and couples. To my husband Jack Fahey, who has always been my biggest fan throughout my career and a constant support.

To Cara: Thank you for your perseverance in the writing of this book and for the commitment you have to both the sex addict and the partner. Writing *Intimate Treason* has been a respectful journey that has always put the experience and the healing potential for the partner first and foremost. It is an understatement to say this book is "thought-felt," as "every" word was given consideration. We worked hard and I appreciate you and your work.

## FROM BOTH OF US

A special thank you to Sandi Klein, Claudia's assistant of many years, who worked diligently helping us to keep moving forward as we collaborated, and who was invaluable in the preparation for the submission to the publishing house. Thank you to Central Recovery Press for believing in the importance of this book.

Lastly, we would like to thank those who have allowed us to be a part of their healing and those of you who will be reading this book and trusting us with the intimacies of your lives.

# INTRODUCTION

Incredible consideration has been given to the journey we're suggesting you embark on as you work through *Intimate Treason.* With a combined fifty years of professional experience, and having worked with hundreds of partners of sex addicts, we have witnessed the journey of men and women who, having experienced profound and often repeated sexual betrayals, have found their voices and regained their self-respect and dignity. We understand the emotional roller coaster you have been on, the tough questions you must somehow answer, and the uncertainty ahead. We also know the strength and courage you have within you. While a few of you may know your inner strength is there, for those of you feeling overwhelmed and beaten down, we only ask you to put one foot in front of the other—to take this journey one step at a time. Some of these steps may seem pretty small considering all that is ahead of you. But if you are willing, we know there is a path out of your pain and toward a greater freedom of inner peace. That path begins with you.

Choosing to read this book means you have been affected by a partner's sexual infidelity. You may have just discovered or have recently been told about the sexual indiscretions, or it may be the first time you have been willing to face this awful truth. Regardless, if you are married or not, gay or straight, you considered the relationship committed and monogamous. You may be devastated or overwhelmed and seeking answers for what to do next. You may want your relationship to work and need to know what to do to protect yourself as you go forward. You may have rationalized your partner's actions and now, as a result, you feel that your life has no direction. You may be reading this book to prevent this from happening to you again in the future. You wonder what signs you might have missed that would have alerted you sooner to the deception. The relationship may be over, but you can't seem to move on from the betrayal and are afraid to begin a new one. It is possible you have already been down this road before in the past with a partner who cheated on you. Now you are questioning what it is about *you* that attracts unavailable partners. Whatever your situation, *Intimate Treason* offers you a path that will support you in your journey out of the pain and heartache and toward greater happiness and relationship satisfaction.

If you believe your partner has only had an affair or two, you may derive benefit from working through many of the exercises in this book; however, our experience is that treatment for an affair is very different from the treatment of sexually addictive behaviors. The therapist not trained to treat sex addiction inadvertently and unknowingly makes the problem worse by not naming and treating this as problematic sexual behavior or addiction. This further invalidates a partner and often the relationship improves superficially, but the problem remains unaddressed. Sadly, the addiction flourishes despite the treatment. If you are someone who has been told it is just an affair and questions whether addiction may apply to your situation, then we encourage you to read further. You will gain understanding of your pain and learn what you can do differently.

## RESPONDING TO BETRAYAL

The betrayal you are experiencing may manifest itself through a variety of sexual behaviors ranging from noncontact acts found in pornography and masturbation, photo swapping, streaming videos, and chat rooms, to contact acts like visiting strip clubs, engaging in prostitution, visiting massage parlors, and having affairs. Affairs may be sexual and/or emotional with people you don't know or with someone very well-known to you. Other types of behavior can include voyeurism, exhibitionism, child pornography, or sexual abuse—all of which could lead to criminal repercussions, public humiliation, and job losses, adding an additional layer of impact to you and your family.

The influence of the Internet on sexual behaviors and attitudes should not be underestimated. While the problem of sexual addiction existed long before the technology boom of the past twenty years, the Internet has accelerated it for many people. Far more individuals are at risk for developing a problem with online pornography simply from the ease and accessibility found on the Internet. Additionally, the abundance of any type of information, from seeking particular types of men, women, or children, to ideal fantasy situations, combined with *perceived* anonymity, has moved the behavior into the privacy and comfort of the home.

Cybersex provides the illusion of control in seeking the perfect object of desire through the use of the computer, since the risks associated with it seem nonexistent. Faster Internet connections have allowed for more immediate access to pornographic material. This has further expanded into the hand-held device industry and has made secret and illicit acts more portable and, at times, untraceable. The fallout of this has meant that more and more people spend exorbitant hours and days at a time online leading to negative work, interpersonal, and familial consequences. Addicts have found that to keep their affairs anonymous, it's far easier to get disposable phones or a separate phone altogether, further reducing the likelihood that they will be tracked.

Finding a sex partner in the recent past usually meant using a computer to search websites, physically going to a venue, or viewing the back pages of certain magazines. Today there are applications on most hand-held devices that allow one to seek out a partner from anywhere Internet access is available. Previously, an addict would have to have a magazine or book to view porn. Now with a hand-held device or tablet, he or she can view material while in a plane, in a train, or in a car while waiting for the kids after school.

As you struggle to gather some control over what is happening, you are likely to experience contradictory thoughts and feelings about your partner's actions. On the one hand, you can see how completely out of control he or she is and may not even recognize the person you once knew. On the other hand, you can't understand why he or she just doesn't stop the behavior that is destroying the relationship and affecting the entire family. Worse, you blame yourself and think you weren't enough to keep him or her happy or were too naive to recognize what was going on.

Perhaps you recognize this is addiction and you're reading this book to work on yourself and the issues that led to being involved with an unavailable partner. You have been able to separate yourself emotionally from the addict and can see the addiction as his or her own. Or you can accept that there is much you will never know or understand. You are in an exploratory place of wanting to search for the causes and influences that led to your choice of a partner and are focused on what you can do to heal your pain. Or you are not the least bit resolved about what you have been told and question whether there are more secrets and details being withheld from you. That may mean you are experiencing a lot of fear and anxiety, and find yourself still preoccupied by your partner's behaviors. Regardless of what has happened in your relationship, your willingness to read this book and to complete the exercises in it speaks to your strength and desire to take care of yourself and begin the process of healing.

## LANGUAGE AND LABELS

Having your intimate world turned upside down challenges you to confront immediate and long-term fears. Along with these fears you encounter a new language intended to describe the behavior and attributes of addicts and their partners. Sometimes that language can feel stigmatizing and invalidating, especially for partners who can be made to feel responsible for the actions of the addict.

Our intention with the labeling in this book is to help identify common themes and pathways individuals take on the road to recovery, as well as what is helpful to you to find your own voice and speak from that place of truth. We also believe that language offers a framework, a road map of sorts, to direct you in recovery and along a path that has proven helpful to others who walked this path before you. Not everyone is alike and despite the commonality you may find in reading others' stories, your journey is yours alone to make. A label is intended to bring meaning and context to your circumstances, and in that way empower you in your decision making.

We believe we would be remiss if we didn't point out the markers, pitfalls, and common tendencies that many partners share in their journey to finding wholeness. For this reason, we see it as essential to have a common language in which to name things. Having a place where words and language are used to describe what you've been experiencing is tremendously validating as you navigate these turbulent waters of addiction.

We work clinically from a model based on addiction and trauma. We see addiction as defined by the person who no longer demonstrates control over the frequency of his or her sexual behaviors; whose behavior demonstrates a cyclical pattern with established rituals; maintains secrets related to behaviors; and continues with those behaviors despite adverse consequences to him- or herself and others. Our focus is on *you*, the loved one, to help raise awareness of the problem, foster safety where you can explore your pain, and offer hope that healing is possible. Primarily, we intend to do this by validating and bringing meaning to the trauma of intimate betrayal—a real, profound, and pervasive experience that has caused serious pain. Addressing this is the **first** priority. We believe that to label this anything but trauma is devaluing to you and your pain and can make accessing appropriate care more difficult at a time when it is so needed. Symptoms of trauma can also be mistaken for codependency, but to treat them as such further traumatizes you. It is our goal to help you accept and validate the trauma, and in time develop the ability to ferret out those codependent traits that also interfere with your ongoing healing.

Based on our experience observing partners confront and heal from their crises, we believe that both your pain and the constellation of your symptoms are traumatic and codependent, not either/or. Codependency is often a condition that exists for many partners who have found themselves in these types of relationships. It is these codependent traits and behaviors that you may have brought to the relationship as part of your reaction to addiction, even when addiction was unknown to you. These behaviors are self-defeating and contribute to low self-esteem.

As you address the trauma of addictive sexual behavior you will begin to peel back the layers of coping skills that were ineffective in the relationship and that compromised your self-worth. You will explore areas of the relationship where you over- and/or under-functioned and begin to see this as both trauma response and traits of codependency. You will reflect on who you were in the relationship prior to any awareness of your partner's sexual acting out. It is at this point the characteristics of codependency may make more sense to you and you may see how they served to protect you from facing other painful truths about yourself and your partner.

We believe this book will help you determine "first things first," which means looking at your crisis concerns versus long-term difficulties in relationships that preceded the addiction. To realistically recover from sexual betrayal we invite you to explore patterns that led to trusting an untrustworthy person. Our intention is not to blame you for someone else's behavior, but rather to encourage self-reflection and understanding for how you got here.

## YOUR JOURNEY: SPEAKING YOUR TRUTH ABOUT LIVING WITH SEX ADDICTION

There are an increasing number of books that present a framework for understanding the complexity of sex addiction and its impact on the couple; but there are few that speak directly to the partners. While Claudia has written a powerful book that offers a framework for your recovery, *Deceived: Facing Sexual Betrayal, Lies, and Secrets*, and Cara has addressed particular themes partners confront in *Mending a Shattered Heart*, what differentiates *Intimate Treason* from others is that this is *your* story and it is centered around what has occurred, what is happening now, and what you need to help you move through the fear, anger, and uncertainty that results from a relationship with a sex addict. We guide you through a process that allows you to both share and explore your own narrative, fears, ambiguity, and hopes, and discover the answers residing within you.

This is written as a workbook, which means you need a pen or pencil and a journal. Whatever you choose to use, be it a book of blank pages, or a lined notebook, or a computer, this journal will hold your feelings and thoughts, and ultimately, your direction. When you work the exercises in *Intimate Treason*, set aside a specific time and place where you can be focused, with as little disruption as possible. Find a comfortable spot and begin your healing process.

We have placed this icon throughout the book to direct you to write in your journal. We want you to have the space to write as little or as much as you find helpful. Your personal journal allows for that. Depending on your daily life and your style of processing information about yourself, you may engage in writing daily, a few times a week, or only on weekends. We encourage you to find support, but if you can already identify a person whom you trust, be it a therapist or dear friend, you may want to let him or her know you are entering a period of self-discovery through this book.

Chapter One, "Claiming My Reality," sets the foundation for your recovery and is meant to offer validation of your pain. You will have a structure with which to begin to tell your story, the opportunity to explore the language that may be new to you, the chance to examine the overall impact the sexual behaviors have had on your life, and most importantly, you will have access to tools with which to feel greater stability.

Chapter Two, "Turning Inward," builds on the foundation you are now establishing and acknowledges the uncertainty you are experiencing. It contains exercises that will teach you how to safely walk through the grieving process. Chapter Two will show you how to stay physically and emotionally grounded during a time in which you may feel disconnected from yourself. It also helps you recognize your inner strengths as you discover reasons to be hopeful for yourself.

Chapter Three, "My Part of the Dance," focuses on the core issues you need to take ownership of that relate to your part of the relationship. Emotional defenses and reactions are addressed as well as unhealthy patterns. It will also help you look at primary behavioral problems common to partners while providing you the opportunity to learn healthier ways of relating.

Chapter Four, "Recognizing the Role of Childhood Influences," examines the beliefs and behaviors you internalized and learned growing up that have affected your relationships today. These patterns lead to self-defeating behaviors and set you up for unsatisfying intimate relationships. By framing some of the themes from childhood that helped to shape you, you will begin to see what is maladaptive today and what offers direction for personal change.

Chapter Five, "Taking Charge of Your Life," shows you how to strengthen and build upon the skills addressed in the previous chapters. It will address a variety of immediate concerns and offer problem-solving ideas. Chapter Five sets the stage for moving forward as you become empowered to integrate and practice these skills in all of your relationships.

The last chapter, "Moving Forward," offers exercises to solidify your recovery plans and set goals for yourself. It also helps you to consider forgiveness and its timing in your healing. It is important to know what forgiveness means to you so you can come to terms with how it does or does not fit into your recovery process at this time. Further in this chapter you will have an opportunity to explore the meaning and role of spirituality. We have seen more women and men deepen their recovery when they have incorporated a spiritual dimension in their healing that is right for them, and we encourage you to explore what that is or might look like for you.

At the time you pick up this book we know you are struggling and looking for answers. You may think the answers lie in what your partner or future partner will do; will he or she act out again; can you ever trust him or her? Our goal in writing this book is to help you see that the answers lie within you. We believe *you* have the power to affect your own behavior, and create choices in how you wish to live your life going forward. This book is meant to help *you* regain your self-respect.

By taking this life-changing step in your willingness to not just read, but *do* the exercises in this book, it is our hope that *Intimate Treason* will be a piece of your journey. Although an important piece, we realize healing cannot occur only through a book. Ultimately, it must involve sharing with others and making changes. Whatever emerges from these pages for you, we hope it will spur you on toward additional support and help from others knowledgeable about partners of sex addicts. Some of you may have already reached out for professional assistance or sought out self-help or personal resources. For others, this workbook may be your initial step toward healing. You start where you can. We are simply grateful and consider it an honor to walk with you in this part of your healing.

There is an ancient prayer—

*"I step into the day, I step into the night;*
*I step into the mystery."*

You have begun; you have stepped into the mystery.
You are on a journey and where it takes you is yet to be
revealed, but what we do know is it can only help you to
heal your pain, offer you a path that generates clarity, and
empower you in all aspects of your life.

# CHAPTER ONE

# Claiming My Reality

This chapter sets the foundation for your recovery and offers validation for what has occurred and the effect it has had on you. We will gently guide you to create the space needed to voice your sorrow and pain as you acknowledge the reality of your current situation. Putting pen to paper will help disperse the thoughts and feelings that overwhelm you—understandably, in response to the trauma you're facing. We will also help you explore earlier suspicions and understand how you were misled and what you can do to acknowledge and act on suspicions in the future. These insights and strategies will assist you in repairing your mistrust of yourself and regain confidence going forward. We offer tools to help you feel more stable, and encourage you to reach out and utilize those available support systems.

# Telling My Story: The Day My World Changed

*This section gives you an opportunity to write about the impact of being deceived by your partner's sexually compulsive behaviors. You will compile a cohesive picture and timeline of what has occurred based on your experience. By writing your narrative, you give voice to your pain and recognize how you coped, perhaps allowing compassion for yourself to begin to emerge. Your story shows how much you trusted the addict over yourself and begins the process of developing an internal boundary where you separate your truth from your partner's.*

One of the most important first steps in healing from this personal crisis is telling your story. It begins with the crisis and how you've been lied to. Living with addiction means your truth is often skewed to fit the reality of the addict, regardless of whether you knew addiction existed or not. The purpose of this exercise is to validate what has happened by helping you tell your story. Narrating what happened and the impact it had on you becomes your truth of all that has occurred. It lays bare your voice; important, powerful, and freeing, since it is no one else's truth but your own. You may have told no one the full story. Possibly you have had to share pieces of it so as to not bring more pain and embarrassment to yourself.

Narrating your story gives a beginning and an end to what has occurred. It reveals in a more concrete way all that you have gone through. The pieces of the story have been just that—pieces, scattered like a mosaic or puzzle without any shape or definition. Telling what happened becomes a way to make real perhaps what has not felt as real as now.

Writing down your story has many benefits, as it

- Creates emotional distance by separating you from the problem.
- Offers validation of the facts and the pain caused to you by your partner's lies.
- Provides a context for understanding why he or she wrongly blamed you for his or her moods and/or actions.
- Honors the need to express what has happened to you.
- Gives permission to leave a piece of the pain behind.
- Separates you from your partner's actions.

Following are questions pertaining to the events leading up to and including how you learned that you were being lied to. The questions are designed to allow you to trace back to the beginning when you discovered the behaviors. Often a place to start is the day you learned something that irreparably altered what you had previously believed or thought. Usually this is considered the *crisis event*—a day like no other, for it was the catalytic moment that prompted you to face your partner's behaviors in a way you never had before. For some, this event extends over a few days or weeks.

**EXAMPLES**

*While driving home from a work trip, I got a call from my husband, but he wasn't calling to talk. He had inadvertently phoned me, and as I listened, I heard him talking to another woman. Then I heard them going to a hotel room and eventually I listened to them having sex. Although before this time I feared he might have had an affair, it was this phone call that changed everything between us. It's been two years and I still can't stop thinking about what I heard that day.*

· · · ·

*It was a week before our tenth anniversary. It's a date I will never forget. I don't know what to call the day—an anniversary?*

· · · ·

*Right after Thanksgiving 2006, I noticed my husband was taking the dog for walks every evening, something he never did before. He would take his cell phone with him. So when he was asleep one night I checked his call log and called the number that he'd called while walking the dog. A woman answered and I hung up. I decided not to do anything until after the holidays. In January, I hired a detective to follow him on a trip to Washington and found he was having an affair with an escort. I confronted him with the facts and told him I had gone to see an attorney who recommended that I see a therapist.*

- What was the date and day of the crisis event? If there is more than one, then focus on the day and date that has the most significance to you now.

- Where were you and was anyone else around? Was it a public or private place?

- Describe what happened.

**EXAMPLES**

*I was visiting a friend who lived two hours from my home and I checked my email to find one from a woman telling me she was having an affair with my husband. I sat there in disbelief. I was stunned and then I got into his email account and found hundreds of emails from this woman and several others. I didn't know what to do. My friend's kids were eating breakfast and I couldn't tell my friend what I just learned. I called my husband and told him I needed to see him at home and the tone of my voice must have scared him because he said he'd meet me there in two hours. I drove home and it was the longest drive of my life! To this day, I still have no idea how I got home. I was shaking and crying and nearly drove off the road.*

· · · ·

*My husband and I had been in couples' therapy and I suspected my husband was having an affair. He denied it repeatedly. One day I signed in to check my email and he had left his email account open. I found emails from three different women. I printed out those emails. I now had facts to back up my suspicions.*

- What can you recall about the rest of that day?

- How did you respond or react upon learning what your partner had done?

- What were you feeling emotionally and physically when you learned of your partner's behaviors that day?

- Is there anything you wish you could have said or done differently on that day?

**EXAMPLE**

*I remember confronting my husband and telling him he had to leave. It was evening. I was alone, and I sat at the kitchen table and cried and cried. I was so scared, but I knew he couldn't stay in the house after what he'd done. It was the first time I was ever alone since being a child.*

When you think of that day there may have been signs or prior circumstances that had you questioning your partner's actions. Describe prior circumstances and/or events where you had suspicions and his or her behavior was called into question.

**EXAMPLES**

*Ten years ago I found a list of phone numbers in my husband's wallet. It made no sense so I called a few and found out that these were women and/or men, who, when I asked who they were, hung up.*

. . . .

*From the time we started dating, I knew my husband was looking at porn. I thought all men did this so I didn't mind. But last year I came across a website where he had been chatting with other women and then learned he met a woman from another part of the country. He had been lying to me and cheating with other women.*

As you recall the memories of that day it may bring up prior events that had you second guessing and suspecting your partner's behavior and you now realize you were probably right. That too is a part of your story. As you are flooded with memories of the past, you often gain greater clarity about the present, even though it may raise additional questions and cause you painful, scary, and uncertain feelings. You have been denied the truth—truth you had a right to know. Writing your part of the story helps you claim your experience.

## My Suspicions Realized

*Now you will focus on identifying those sexual behaviors, situations, or attitudes that represent your partner's acting out. In this exercise you identify those times where warning signs, suspicions, or triggers were known to you and the ways you did or did not respond. This helps you examine how you were betrayed and deceived—often by half-truths, blatant lies, or avoidant responses thereby hampering your ability to react appropriately at the time. You will also come to recognize how you became unknowingly complicit in the acting out.*

*By understanding these patterns, both of the addict and yourself in ignoring, denying, or overreacting to a suspicion, you will learn new ways to handle suspicions and come to trust yourself. Recognizing how suspicions were ignored often provides you with some understanding as to the development of the addictive behavior. It also empowers you to move forward with your healing.*

Coming to terms with the sexual and emotional behaviors of the addict is an enormous part of what confronts you. The sexual behaviors may feel offensive, abnormal, and wrong. Learning that he or she saw prostitutes or had a long-term affair(s) has you incensed and outraged.

"How could he do this?" "What's wrong with her?" "What's wrong with me?" are obvious questions that run through your mind.

When you are bombarded by the images of what you found out, working through your pain seems like a tall order. Wishing you could shut out the visual images that now plague you or turn back time to when you still trusted your partner is a normal response to the trauma of intimate betrayal. You will probably experience a flood of thoughts, feelings, and new beliefs or hunches as you work to make sense of all the data. Perhaps you are someone who would rather not think of it at all and find that you stay busy and feel numb as a way to avoid the pain.

What you have learned is now a part of your story. In the beginning, the urge to know can be overwhelming and you may find yourself searching for additional facts to substantiate what you already know. Your distress and turmoil mixed with the facts of all he or she did makes you feel as though the pain and confusion will never end. You have a right to know what has occurred and what may be occurring now. Yet searching for more information and trying to clarify what is known is making you feel worse because it draws you further into the morass of the behaviors. Perhaps all this searching is an attempt to come to terms with how little control you had over everything that was withheld from you. Searching is more an attempt at self-protection and a traumatic response to how duped you were by the secrets in the past.

The list below identifies categories of behaviors in which sex addicts engage. In your journal, write down all that apply to your partner.

- Masturbation.
- Flirting.
- Voyeurism and/or staring too long at other people.
- Frequenting strip clubs.
- Affairs—sexual, emotional.
- Hiring prostitutes/escorts.
- Phone sex.
- Cybersex—viewing porn, chat rooms, online to offline activity.
- Demanding sex from you.
- Viewing porn on DVDs, video streaming on phone, computer, TV.
- Other.


- Write down your feelings as you went through the above list.

- Did the checklist trigger any suspicions or old memories? Describe.


## HINDSIGHT: WARNING SIGNS MISSED

While you may not have known about the sexual behaviors, most likely there were other signs that indicated something was wrong in your relationship. These can be behaviors or activities where addiction was operating, unknown to you. They are patterns that show up in the tasks of daily living that are often ineffectively addressed and over time become chronic. In a relationship where secrets and lies exist, these patterns represent the missing link, the hidden piece of the puzzle from which to draw. You couldn't know what was kept hidden unless accidentally stumbling across it or being told.

The sexual behaviors were secret and meant to be so. But it is often those other areas where problems existed that will help you reflect on how you quieted your misgivings and doubts, or instead attempted to rehash your concerns/complaints in order to change your partner—all to no avail. Reflecting on these areas will offer you a window into where warning signs existed. Perhaps there was a pattern of allowing his or her reasoning to trump your own or believing that his or her complaints about you somehow justified the actions in some way. Coming to your own aid is discovering how you missed or possibly disregarded the warning signs. Identifying incidents and hunches becomes useful in learning to trust your own judgment as you move forward with the healing process.

The following are examples of warning signs that problem areas existed. In your journal, list all those that you now recognize may have been signs for you.

- Sex—avoidance of sex, high demand for sex, novelty or wanting to try out new techniques.

- Communication—avoiding conflict, avoiding specific topics, blaming behavior.

- Time away from family through work.

- Excessive extracurricular activity.

- Imbalance in household responsibilities.

- Finances—kept secret, one person in control of all assets, money unaccounted for, unexplained debt.

- Chronic lateness.

- Physically or emotionally absent from children.

- Fighting without resolution.

- Protracted periods of silence or willful emotional withholding by the addict.

- Coercive behavior—control, anger.

- Underperformance at work—job losses or little advancement in career.

- Repeated moves due to change in work or lifestyle pursuits.

- Change in social behavior—avoiding friends, activities.

- Other.

## DISCOUNTING YOUR PERCEPTIONS

In addition to warning signs, you may have overheard or seen something that caused you to be suspicious.

### EXAMPLE

*Ten years ago I found list of phone numbers in my husband's wallet. I called the people and either didn't reach them or they hung up on me. I went to my husband and told him I knew he was seeing other women and here was the list of names. He told me he loved me, that it wasn't what I thought it was. He acted so outraged that I would ever doubt him and flatly denied he lied or would ever lie to me.*

- List three incidents where you had suspicions. For each incident describe what happened, what you did or didn't do, and your thoughts and feelings at the time.

- If you did not act on your suspicions, what did you tell yourself in order to quiet your doubts?

### EXAMPLES

*I told myself that was stupid thinking and wondered what was wrong with me; he wouldn't do that.*

. . . .

*I told myself I was just a jealous type.*

. . . .

*I told myself I had to think only positive and loving thoughts.*

. . . .

*I told myself he wouldn't hurt me or the kids.*

Sex addicts are masters of deception. They need this to support and maintain the behaviors not only to keep you from knowing, but also to avoid facing the truth about themselves. Whether deception is done through manipulating you with charm, bullying, or persuasion, it is also driven by a need to deflect you from the truth of what they are doing. Considering the deception being kept from you, it is understandable that you allowed behaviors and explanations by your partner to sway you against your better judgment and intuition.

Did you allow your suspicions to be changed or swayed by the addict? Explain.

## THAT WHICH HURTS THE MOST

Some aspects of what you learned he or she did are more traumatizing and painful than others.

### EXAMPLES

*His having sex with men. This was, and still is, the hardest part for me.*

. . . .

*When I discovered my husband had been having sex with other women I thought I would die. But when I learned one of the women was my boss that was devastating to me. We eventually divorced because the damage from that personal relationship was too great, and I knew I could never trust him again.*

. . . .

*She had an affair with our son's fifth grade soccer coach. That was bad enough, but then she got pregnant by him. It has brought such embarrassment and shame to our family.*

For some of you, it is the blatant lying when you confronted him or her or the loss of trust that is most hurtful. Recognizing that all of it is painful, identify that which hurts the most. Of all that you learned, what do you believe will be the hardest to overcome and why?

By taking the time to answer these questions, you may feel more exposed and find you are flooded with memories that cause you to question everything about your past with your partner. Be patient and recognize that this is a response to the trauma of betrayal. Writing down your story clarifies your journey and further underscores the wrongs done to you. It also points out how you discounted, ignored, and/or minimized suspicions or doubts. Reasons for why you may have done this, although identified here, will be further explored later in the book.

There is no good time to be confronted with something of this magnitude, but we have worked with many betrayed partners, who, when faced with this deception, found they could—one day at a time—find the necessary strength and fortitude to face what was in front of them. The fact that you are reading this book demonstrates a desire to move out of the pain you are experiencing, even if it means unearthing buried or forgotten memories from the past. This is a sign of courage.

## Grappling with the Language of Sex Addiction

*Here is an opportunity to reflect on the language of sexual addiction and its impact on you. The words pertaining to addiction can be confusing, possibly offensive or frightening, or they may immediately offer something that makes sense and provides clarity. It is important to explore these meanings for yourself.*

What comes to mind when you hear the term "sex addict?" In your journal, write down any of the descriptors below if you think it means the person:

- Is perverted.
- Is amoral.
- Has a weak character.
- Is a molester.
- Is a monster.
- Has no control over his or her sexual behavior.
- Is bad.
- Is just like (name) _____ (mother/father/other significant person in my life) and that means _____.
- Is wounded.
- Needs help.
- Has an addiction to sex, just like to alcohol and/or other drugs.

Sex and addiction are two words that conjure judgments and varying associated beliefs. While there is a wide spectrum of behaviors that encompass what is and what is not normal sexual expression, sex and sexuality often mean different things to different people. How we form our understanding of sex and sexuality is shaped by the social, cultural, and religious beliefs of our time. Further, how our families addressed sex affects the way sex becomes viewed and experienced by us.

Various fields of study address the function, meaning, and normative versus non-normative sex and sexuality. Psychology has been heavily influenced by Sigmund Freud, who believed that our libido is driven by our sexual urges and is often not in our control since much of this stems from the unconscious. The world of literature, as well as the music industry, has contributed much to forming and maintaining the notion that the romantic view of sex is a natural expression of true love.

Religion has strongly influenced the role of sex to be specifically about procreation. For centuries there have been major differences regarding the expectations and norms for men and women. For women, sex has been strongly related to love and connection; for men, it has been more of a pleasurable physical act; and for some men (and women), it is about power and control.

The "sexual revolution" of the 1960s and 1970s brought with it cultural and social changes that freed people to have sex outside of a committed relationship. The advent of the birth control pill, and later the legalization of abortion, ameliorated the consequences of unwanted pregnancies and gave women permission to be sexual. With the introduction of the home video, the pornography industry started to boom. Marketing to middle-class males made viewing porn more of a socially acceptable activity. Social mores were changing. Magazines like *Playboy*, *Penthouse*, and *Hustler* become household names as the three competed for market share.

The growth of pornography expanded further with the explosion of the Internet in the 1990s and continues into the present. Accessing and viewing porn is now easier as other electronic forms of obtaining and exchanging information have become available. This has further normalized the viewing of porn, as well as expanded the variety of avenues sexual interest and behavior can be pursued. In many ways, pornography in the technological age has lessened the importance of human touch, and enables a sexuality devoid of attachment to others.

Similar contradictions and polarizing views can be seen in defining addiction. Historically, addiction to substances like alcohol and other drugs was perceived as moral decay and weakness of character. For many it is still seen as such and thought of as a lack of willpower or self-discipline. In the 1930s, a group of men got together to address their alcoholism and formed the first twelve-step group called Alcoholics Anonymous (AA). The growth of AA led to professionals beginning to see this as a treatable problem and the terms "disease" and "addiction" were coined. By the 1950s the World Health Organization (WHO), a leader in helping countries create unity in identifying and treating social ills, also began to view addiction as a disease with defining characteristics and resulting consequences. From the 1960s to the 1990s much attention turned to the disease model, as well as the role families played in enabling the problem and what they could do to change for themselves despite living with someone else's addiction.

Today much focus, in both research and treatment, has been in the area of brain science. In the 1990s the then director of the National Institute on Drug Abuse (NIDA) at the National Institute of Health (NIH), Alan Leshner, PhD, coined the term "brain disease." Brain science is lending a tremendous amount of effort and research to verifying how changes occur in the brain with use of substances and behaviors like drugs and sex.

Over thirty years ago, Patrick Carnes, PhD, was the first to generalize what was known about addiction to alcohol and other drugs (substances) and apply it to sexual behavior. The pioneering work of Milkman and Sunderwirth strengthened the foundation to broaden the understanding of addiction beyond substances to behavior. While there is increasing agreement among the body of treatment professionals and recovery communities from various manifestations of addiction, for the lay person and the masses living in our neighborhoods and communities across the country and world, there is still a major discord in the beliefs about what addiction is and what to call it.

Consequently, to combine sex with addiction, the term "sex addiction" is at best, confusing. For many, it is offensive and frightening; for others, it offers clarity and direction. Is this term new for you? Has anyone told you that they thought your partner was a sex addict? Have you wondered that yourself? Have you done any online tests trying to assess whether or not it is addiction? Have you found yourself reading books that explain sex addiction? After reviewing the descriptors at the beginning of this exercise, do you believe any of these apply to your partner?

- Take a moment to pause and breathe, and then write down what you think of when you hear the term "sex addict."

- Describe your partner's behavior and whether you believe the behavior is addictive.

- Explain what makes you think your partner is or is not a sex addict. If you are not sure, what is contributing to your uncertainty?

**EXAMPLES**

*He is a sex addict. He uses sex as he used drugs, and he was clearly addicted to the drugs.*

. . . .

*He is a sex addict because he knows his pornography is hurting our marriage and yet he keeps going back to it. He can't stop on his own, and I actually think he wants to stop.*

. . . .

*I don't think she's a sex addict. To my knowledge she has only had two affairs in fifteen years and both were one night stands when she was on the road. I think she was angry with me and getting back at me.*

. . . .

*I'm not sure. I know he had sexual secrets with his last partner, but he says it is not addictive and he can stop. I want to believe him.*

Taking into account the circumstances that have led you to confront sexual addiction and the social, cultural, and religious climate that has influenced and shaped your world, it is important to acknowledge what the words addiction and sex addiction mean to you. By doing so you further engage in a process of defining and owning your experience.

# The Ripple Effect: Cost of Addiction in My Life

*This section will help you become aware of the pervasive impact addiction has had on you. You will identify those areas most affected. Reflecting on relationships, both personal and social, your parenting, your work, and the emotional and physical toll on yourself will give clarity as to the extent of the problem. It will also help you prioritize that which is most critical for you to address in order to establish and maintain safety in this early phase of your recovery.*

You are coming to terms with information that either validates your suspicions or has taken you totally by surprise. It has shaken the foundation of your relationship, spilling over into other areas of your life. This exercise is focused on the crisis at hand—the triggering event(s) or situation(s)—that altered the course of the relationship and has you reaching for help in new ways. The following questions guide you to explore the most immediate problems facing you by identifying those areas affected and recognizing the extensive effect addiction is having on your life. It will help you to prioritize and label those critical concerns.

## RELATIONSHIP

How has your relationship been affected?

**EXAMPLES**
*He calls me from work every hour saying he is just checking in when in the past he never called at all. I find myself confused. I am angry and rude toward him, and yet, sort of relieved.*

. . . .

*She keeps telling me it is me she wants, not those other men, and she doesn't need to go for help, she can handle it. I walk away from her when she tells me that, or I start to rage at her. Either way I feel sick.*

- You may very likely be screaming (literally or figuratively) that you need answers and you want to know how this situation is going to be resolved and what the outcome will be for your relationship. Do you have any immediate relationship concerns?

## EMOTIONAL

How has your emotional life been affected?

**EXAMPLES**

*I am crying all of the time. I cry at work, in the car, watching TV, in bed. I can't seem to stop.*

. . . .

*I'm a walking zombie. I can't concentrate. I can't listen. Then I suddenly burst into tears. This all happens while I am out shopping, taking the kids to school, or at the health club. I am a mess.*

- You may very likely feel like you are on an emotional roller coaster. Perhaps you are the offender or the recipient of threats, verbal rage, outbursts, belittling, intimidation, etc. Do you have any immediate emotional concerns?

## SOCIAL

How has your social life been affected?

**EXAMPLES**

*He doesn't want to go do anything, and I don't want to stay at home with him.*

. . . .

*Our social life has not changed, but I realize how living this lie is such a farce with our so-called friends not knowing. We pretend all is okay, and I spend my whole time being quietly angry. People ask me what is wrong, but I am too ashamed to say anything and my wife acts like everything is fine.*

- You may think that your social life is the least of your concerns, but for some there may be very intense situations such as being some place socially where you expect to encounter someone with whom your partner has acted out. Do you have any immediate social concerns?

## SEXUAL

How has your sexual relationship been impacted?

**EXAMPLES**

*Actually, per the therapist's suggestion, we aren't having sex for a while. And that makes it easier.*

. . . .

*I find myself obsessing about what he has done while we are being sexual.*

• Concerns could be something such as engaging in unprotected sex or being physically forced or verbally coerced to engage in sexual practices you do not want. Do you have any immediate sexual concerns?

## PARENTAL

How has the parenting of your children been affected?

**EXAMPLES**

*I find myself distracted and not listening to my kids. They are reacting to us by being more whiny and needy. My young one has started to wet the bed again.*

. . . .

*I have had to send them to my mother's for the time being. I talk to them on the phone or pick them up after school for a while.*

• If you have children, your situation does not necessarily create an immediate crisis for them. While the possibility certainly exists, there are some circumstances where immediate considerations are indicated such as whether or not there are safety concerns regarding you and/or the children. Do you have any immediate parenting concerns?

## PHYSICAL

How has your physical well-being been impacted?

**EXAMPLES**

*I have started to have migraines.*

. . . .

*I've gained weight/I've lost weight.*

• Abuse is absolutely an immediate concern, such as hitting, shoving, slapping, throwing objects, being locked up, etc. Do you have any immediate physical concerns?

## EMPLOYMENT

How has your work performance been impacted?

**EXAMPLES**

*I have told too many people at work and now I am embarrassed.*

. . . .

*I have taken a lot of time off work saying I am sick.*

• Typically any work crisis involves the one acting out, but you may be experiencing work-related problems due to poor performance or frequent absenteeism. Do you have any immediate work concerns?

## FINANCES

How have your finances been affected?

**EXAMPLES**

*He has spent $50,000 on prostitutes in eight months, and I have started to hide money as a form of self-protection.*

. . . .

*We needed to hire an attorney and had to cash in some stocks in order to do that.*

• Frequently there are concerns of the possibility of secret bank accounts, hidden credit cards, the cost of therapy or treatment, or the cost of living separately, etc. Do you have any immediate financial concerns?

## LEGAL

Have there been legal problems?

**EXAMPLES**

*We had to retain attorneys for the sexual harassment suit from his affair with his partner at work, and then we had to retain a criminal attorney to defend him in court.*

. . . .

*There has been some stalking so we had to get a restraining order against one of his girlfriends.*

• There are frequently legal concerns, such as pending or threatened civil or criminal suits, ethics violations, paternity concerns, etc. Do you have any immediate legal concerns?

## SPIRITUAL

How has your spiritual life been impacted?

**EXAMPLES**

*I am so angry at God—there is no spiritual life for me.*

. . . .

*I realize I don't use the fellowship of my church for any support.*

- If there is a spiritual crisis it may be more internal, such as questioning whether or not there is a God. But it may also be more tangible and you question the conflict of attending or seeking guidance in your house of worship because the acting out may be related to people in the congregation or even the clergy. Is there a threat of excommunication? Do you have any immediate spiritual concerns?

Doing this exercise will help you see the pervasiveness of addiction, that is, the ripple effect. Most likely there is no part of your life that has been left untouched. At this stage what is important is to identify and prioritize that which requires your most immediate attention. By stopping the "bleeding" and focusing your energy on those areas you listed, you will become better equipped to move forward and begin the healing process.

## Managing Triggers

*This exercise is designed to identify how you've been responding to the trauma of being betrayed. It will help you identify and, more importantly, cope with triggers. Triggers are those situations, activities, or behaviors that often, though not always, remind you of the sexual acting out. Once you are triggered, it often becomes difficult to distinguish between the reality of today and the cascade of emotions and memories reminiscent of the traumatic experience of betrayal. You will look at some of the ways these triggers, when not managed, can lead to self-sabotaging actions. We will offer tools and resources to help lessen the intensity of your feelings and the behaviors and provide you with choices in how to respond in a healthy manner.*

During this time of upheaval you may feel emotionally out of control. You're preoccupied all the time and wish you could turn off the thoughts that plague you day and night. These are typical responses to overwhelming trauma. Many betrayed partners describe feeling trapped and vulnerable. The preoccupation is also a symptom of the intimate trauma as the intrusive memories remind you of what you've learned. They are daily reminders of what you are coping with today. These are referred to as *triggers.*

Triggers can be events, situations, sensory memories, and/or circumstances that remind you of the addiction and send warning signals that you might be in danger. Triggers can reflect a real or imagined threat, but foremost they are a learned response to the original trauma of discovery/disclosure. Without developing tools to handle these triggers, you will be unprepared to handle and effectively address situations with your spouse/partner today. When a trigger occurs, you are reminded again of the lack of control you experienced at the time of the betrayal. The feeling is overpowering, and you may be afraid that your emotions will overcome you or compel you to behave in ways you may later regret. At such a vulnerable time, reacting to how you feel can often have risks to you or others since it's created from an impulse and a desire to eradicate the pain you are experiencing.

**EXAMPLES**

*The day after confronting my boyfriend about an affair I discovered he was having, and his agreeing to see a counselor with me, I called him at work and he's not where he said he would be. I get in the car and check out every hotel I can locate within a fifteen mile radius. It took me three hours. I get home and there he is; he had been in a car accident. Because of the mental frenzy I was in, I totally forgot that I needed to be at school for an appointment regarding my daughter. He was apologetic, but it was clearly a reaction to what I'd just learned that drove the frenzy. I felt the only way to quell my fear was to track him down.*

. . . .

*I am just consumed with the details of what I have learned and I wanted everyone to know what a b\*@#%$^ he is. I sent out emails to everyone on my Facebook and Twitter accounts telling them in detail what I had just learned. I left nothing out.*

. . . .

*A week after I am confronted with my wife's behavior, I am on a work trip, and this woman flirts with me and makes it clear she has an interest in me, so I thought "my wife has been doing this for years, it's my turn." So I did.*

Having fantasies of revenge is absolutely normal; acting on them is not. Wishing that something, anything would take away your pain is understandable. Looking for immediate relief is not. Acting on revenge fantasies in the moment feels so right, and the behavior feels justified and rewarding. Your mind blocks out all other thoughts, your vision becomes narrow, and you forget everything else you know. When you move into a fight response, your body begins to respond by readying you for action through the increase of cortisol, adrenaline, and noradrenalin in the blood stream. This primitive response serves to help you defend against threat, but it also reduces capacity for rational thought, preventing you from anticipating what the consequences of your actions will be. Indulging in revenge thinking gives you a sense of power and control along with the sensation of feeling high, but only temporarily. While some people overreact, others underreact and move into a freeze response.

**EXAMPLES**

*Since I have been aware, actually since I have had suspicions, I just cry. I can't seem to stop. I cry and then sleep. Cry and sleep. I am not good for much at all.*

. . . .

*I go about my day, pretending like everything is just fine, like I don't really know any of this stuff.*

. . . .

*It's been three months since I learned of what he has been doing and I find myself isolating and eating, consuming large quantities of sugar. I simply go through the motions of the day.*

The following is a list of reactions common to betrayed partners after learning about the addiction. In your journal, write down all the items you identify as symptoms of the stress you are encountering.

- Persistently asking questions of your partner.

- Searching for proof, that is, checking his or her cell phone, web history, GPS tracking.

- Uncontrollable episodes of anger and rage.

- Seeking revenge by telling entire family, certain friends, having own affair.

- Deliberately purchasing something to antagonize your partner.

- Willing to do anything sexually.

- Punishing him or her with silence.

- Secretly reading his or her recovery writings.

- Sculpting yourself to be the perfect object of his or her sexual desire, that is, extreme dieting, cosmetic surgery, etc.

- Bingeing on food.

- Self-harm, such as banging head, cutting, burning, etc.

- Compulsively watching television or being on the Internet.

- Sleeping extremely long hours, or throughout the day.

- Avoiding any discussion about what you now know.

- Talking incessantly.

- Continual crying.

- Fearful to bring up what you both know.

- Ruminating, obsessive thinking about what you picture or fantasize he or she did and what it looked like, who the partners were, and/or about revenge.

- Other.

What makes these behaviors problematic is that *they* betray you. If you give in to the urge to exact revenge, you will suffer the consequence of further pain and often the problem for which you sought relief will still be there. In order to begin to lessen the automatic urge to react to a trigger, it is important to know that the body needs time for intense reactivity to subside. This can take fifteen to twenty minutes because the brain becomes flooded with a rush of neurochemical changes that prepare you to fight, flee, or freeze. To control an impulse caused by a triggering event, it is essential you create a plan that can be used anytime, anywhere as soon as your body is giving any sensory signs that you are in danger.

Subtle signs such as a receipt for a cash withdrawal, a sex scene on television, or an inappropriate email written by your partner can trigger realistic fear that he or she is acting out. Having the best strategies in place to handle and address triggers is essential to effectively recovering from your trauma. Here are a few ways to acknowledge and then address the triggers.

## STOP TECHNIQUE

Recognizing your reactivity is the first step in stopping self-defeating behavior. Many have found it helpful, as they catch themselves in the behavior, to visualize themselves writing down or saying the word STOP. Slowly count to ten. Then ask yourself, "If I were to act on my urge right at this moment, would it help me in the long run to find answers to my pain?" Then ask what you can do or say to yourself that would be more helpful.

Other questions to ask yourself are, "What do I need right now? What would help me with my pain?" Recognize that you may not have the answer, but by posing the questions you increase your self-awareness and invite compassion into your healing process. The following sections contain tools for you to consider as a way to manage your distress.

## DISTRACTION STRATEGIES

Create a distraction or an image that slows down your thinking. The following is a list of possible distractions. In your journal, write down those that you have utilized successfully and/or are willing to try.

- Taking a walk.
- Exercising.
- Meditating.
- Listening to calming music.
- Writing in a journal.
- Playing with pets.
- Counting to ten (or one hundred).
- Reading self-help literature.
- Attending a self-help group.

- Reaching out to or seeking out a therapist.
- Checking your reality with a friend or family member or other safe person.
- Other.

## IMAGERY

You may also find it helpful to have an image that you can call upon to slow down your obsessive mental focus.

### EXAMPLES

*Dina pictured a blue-green wave washing over her from head to toe, carrying away any unwanted debris (negative thoughts) and taking it out to sea.*

. . . .

*Eve pictured herself driving very fast as if all the signal lights were green, and then envisioned the lights turning yellow, slowing her thoughts. Then as her thoughts begin slowing down more, all the lights gradually turn red.*

. . . .

*Phil envisioned a small harbor where he has anchored his power boat. The waves lapping against the boat from the wake he created gradually become fainter and fainter and fainter.*

. . . .

*Sandie put her thoughts into a bubble and envisioned that bubble floating off into space. She could see the bubble rising and disappearing.*

Identify an image that works for you—something that will slow the process of obsessive, vengeful thinking and gradually dissipate the thought. Be creative. You can write about an image or draw it or even cut it out of a magazine and paste it into your journal.

While the focus of this chapter is on reactivity and managing triggers, some of you may find it difficult to respond to situations in the moment. Your tendency may be to freeze or go numb during an emotionally charged event. Feelings can seem impossible to experience and identifying needs can be similarly elusive. Sometimes the numb response happens in day-to-day living as you may find it difficult to get through your normal responsibilities. These types of nonreactive responses could also be a sign of depression for which outside help from a mental health practitioner should be sought. Many of the techniques in the "Distraction Strategies" listed earlier in this exercise will also be helpful to you.

You know yourself best, so think about what would be most helpful to you. It may be as basic as preparing a meal, talking to someone about how you're feeling, writing about what you are unwilling to do, going to bed at a regular time, returning phone calls, or showering daily.

Now identify three things you are willing to do. Feel free to add to the list above.

## GROUNDING STATEMENTS

Positive self-talk can be a useful tool to manage the intensity of emotions. Think about messages or affirmations that would be useful to you. Take a look at the following statements and in your journal list all those that you are willing to incorporate into your daily thinking.

- I will get through this.
- This is about his or her behavior, not a statement of my worth and value.
- I won't lose myself in this process.
- I have friends who will be there for me.
- I don't need to know all the answers right now.
- I can trust myself.
- I am worthy.
- My needs are important.
- While I am upset now, I won't always feel this way.
- My feelings are important.
- Other.

Managing your reactivity to the many triggers is pivotal to your recovery work. So many partners find this to be one of the most challenging of all tasks in early recovery. You will most likely find that using these tools will help you when you need it most. At certain times in your healing, a particular technique may be more useful than another. Be open to using them and others that you find helpful. They will make a difference.

## Bottom Lines: Nonnegotiable Boundaries

*These are intended to help you stabilize the immediate crisis of being in a relationship with sex addiction as its center. We will share examples many others have used and provide suggestions to take care of* **you**. *It is an extremely important, initial step in learning how to identify and ask for what you need for your immediate safety. In this exercise you will create a nonnegotiable list of those conditions or circumstances that must be met in order for stability to be achieved in the household.*

Becoming aware of your triggers means you will have to renegotiate boundaries that at one time felt predictable and safe. Since the foundation of the relationship has now become unsettled, part of managing triggers is defining boundaries best suited to your situation. This means establishing nonnegotiables, also referred to as bottom lines. They are essential, if not imperative, in early recovery.

Boundaries are borders—a line between where you end and another begins. Boundaries are sometimes flexible, with room for give-and-take between you and another; and other times fixed, like the boundaries between countries or property lines. Being able to define and act upon your boundaries creates a stronger sense of self. It also assumes you can appreciate the boundaries of others. In this exercise, you will explore a specific type of boundary—the nonnegotiable—that has very little give to it and is usually activated in situations in which personal safety is at risk. More about boundaries in relationships will be covered later in the book.

Whether through ignorance, false trust in the addict, or porous boundaries on your part, you were insulated from the deceptive behaviors. If the crisis is recent and you were unaware of the indiscretions, then the need for nonnegotiables is imperative since betrayal leaves you more vulnerable without certain immediate safeguards. Setting limits is a response to the addict's behavior because of *its impact on you.* Your nonnegotiables say to the addict that "you went too far, and in order for me to feel safe and consider rebuilding trust with you, I will need the following . . . ."

The goal in establishing nonnegotiables is to protect you from being duped again and from living with active addiction. Defining your bottom lines means spelling out exactly what that looks like and projecting into the future as to whether or not you're prepared to act upon them. Not doing so undermines your ability to protect yourself from further harm. To prevent boundary failure and promote personal success, you need to be honest about what you are and are not prepared to do in establishing nonnegotiables.

Pay close attention to the person for whom the boundary is intended and why. Nonnegotiable boundaries need to be for **you**—not to punish your partner, despite the urge or inclination to do so. You set nonnegotiables to honor and protect yourself. "This behavior is unacceptable to me," is a statement of self-respect. By not being at the whim of his or her actions and inactions you're setting the direction of your recovery.

Sometimes nonnegotiables can be perceived as controlling. As you are developing your list of bottom lines, your self-doubt may tell you that what you are asking for isn't justified. Hang in there; this is new territory and common misconceptions happen as you try out new actions that are primarily intended for your well-being and not that of the addict. Although it may feel controlling, the distinction has to do with intention and motivation. If the goal is to stop him or her rather than to protect you, then yes, it can be controlling. But if the goal of the limit is for greater stability, then it is a boundary. Working on nonnegotiables is often best done with the support of others. A counselor, a trusted friend, or a twelve-step support person or sponsor can offer perspectives that will allow you to further think through your intentions and motivations so as to ensure you the most success.

The following are examples of nonnegotiables. You will see what others define as intolerable behavior. You can use this as a guide for yourself.

In your journal, list all the examples that pertain to your relationship with the addict.

- I need you to maintain your aftercare for at least one year.
- I need you to attend twelve-step meetings weekly.
- Work-related travel for the next six months is unacceptable.
- No Internet access without filtering software.

- Assets are to be in my name.

- Money will be handled by me for the next six months.

- I need you to be an open book with all email accounts and cell phone bills.

- I need certain named family members to be told about your addiction.

- No contact with affair partner.

- I will engage with you sexually once we have agreed and completed an abstinence contract and have discussed our readiness with our support people.

- I expect us both to be tested for HIV and other sexually transmitted diseases.

- Strip clubs are not acceptable.

- Computer moved to central location.

- From the examples above and your own situation, make a list of your nonnegotiables and consider what you would gain by following through with them. What would the consequence(s) be for you if you did not have these identified nonnegotiables?

The key to a healthy boundary is being willing to follow through with your bottom line. You have probably made threats in the past that both you and your partner know were not acted upon. Therefore, as you consider what your nonnegotiables are and intend to present them to your partner, you need to be prepared to act on them if they are violated. Your inclination might be to focus on relying on the addict to do his or her part, so you won't have to do yours. But following through on your nonnegotiables is your responsibility and is a part of your recovery. To not follow through means you are enabling the behavior; you are saying the behavior is okay. You are willing to tolerate it. And neither you nor the relationship will change. In fact, it may get worse.

By taking the time to define your nonnegotiables list, you give yourself the opportunity to ensure that your actions and your words will be consistent. One man said if he ever learned his wife had contact with her ex-lover, he would immediately file for custody of their only child. A woman said that if her spouse didn't seek inpatient care should he relapse—and for him relapse meant acting out with a person—she would begin filing for divorce. Another woman said that if her partner violated any of the nonnegotiables and didn't tell her within a specified time period, then separation would occur. In all of these examples, these individuals had to be ready to initiate their plan of action should their partner resume the acting-out behaviors.

Here are some examples of consequences if your nonnegotiables are violated.

- I will leave the marriage/relationship.

- I will gather more data and wait and see.

- I will ask him to discuss my concerns with his support group.

- I will tell her that this is unacceptable to me.

- I will sleep in a different bedroom.

- I will ask him or her to go to residential treatment.

- I will follow up on divorce proceedings.

From your list of nonnegotiables, consider what your follow-up actions will be if the boundaries are violated. What do you believe will help you to follow through on your commitment to yourself as these nonnegotiables become part of your self-care?

**EXAMPLES**

*I will ask my counselor and friends to remind me that I am only enabling the behavior and it will just continue as long as I do that.*

. . . .

*I will remind myself to take care of me now, to do certain recovery-oriented things so if I have to follow through I will have greater strength to do it.*

## WAIT-AND-SEE APPROACH

Your nonnegotiable list needs to take into account the totality of what you are facing and how prepared you are for the actions you will need to take if violations occur. The consequences are dependent on you. They can be small or large depending on the degree of the transgression and the reality of whether or not you are prepared to take action.

The wait-and-see approach doesn't necessarily imply an immediate consequence will occur if a boundary is crossed. It is intended more as an observing stance whereby information is gathered and not responded to. This is especially useful for those who are prone to making threats and need time and distance from the violations.

Sometimes you don't act on the first violation because you want to be sure that the addict won't quickly repair the violation by recognizing it and changing course. One woman learned her partner had stopped going to recovery meetings. When she went to confront him on this as a violation of her boundary, he told her he had already recommitted to his program and he was planning to meet with his sponsor and was going to start attending ninety meetings in ninety days. In this case, he took the initiative to reassure her. This did not deny the fact he'd violated the nonnegotiable. The difference here was acknowledgment and reversing course in a more intensive way that for now brought resolution to her.

One woman's nonnegotiable was that her spouse wear his wedding ring as a condition for the marriage to continue, something he refused to do prior to the discovery, saying it was too tight and it got in the way of his job. When he showed up one day without it on his finger, but rather in his pocket, telling her it got in the way of his driving, this violation of her request was conspicuous and compounded by other violations on her list. This became the final strike and at that point she was prepared to begin the process of separation. Another woman had the same issue and viewed this as a wait-and-see violation. She acknowledged it as something that was a negative sign of his commitment to recovery. Her follow-up consequence focused on herself, discussing it with her support group and identifying to herself and others that a violation of her nonnegotiable had occurred. This is an example of the same behavior, but with two different actions taken.

A major distinction between these two very important boundaries is that the consequences for the one are immediate and directed toward the relationship and the other person, and the consequences for the wait-and-see approach are focused on you. If you make a boundary and it is violated, you identify ahead of time what you will do for *you* that will have a less obvious impact on the other person. "I will be willing to explore with my therapist a therapeutic separation." "I will attend an intensive workshop for partners of sex addicts."

From your list of nonnegotiables, write next to each item whether it is in need of immediate action or would be in a wait-and-see category.

While some of you may want to quickly work on defining your bottom lines, take your time and be certain you are ready for what you are expecting and need. Establishing bottom lines prematurely sets up old patterns of making threats with no follow through (consequences).

Nonnegotiables are to help *you* by creating a safe environment in which you can heal. Although we strongly believe that nonnegotiables are valid and important, we want to underscore that they are best worked through with a counselor. Your therapist will be able to help you clarify boundaries that are best-suited for your situation. You can also get feedback from other recovering partners. They will have a perspective you may not have. If your partner is not pursuing recovery you will want to strategize how you present these limits to him or her. In both cases, it can be helpful to rehearse this conversation ahead of time so you are more confident.

If you are not currently in a relationship, it is still important to know your bottom lines. It gives you a chance to see your vulnerabilities from the past and where you need to focus your attention in relationships as you go forward in recovery. Again, bottom lines are not about punishing, but are about helping you create safety for yourself.

## Deciding Whom to Tell

*This exercise walks you through what you need to consider when you choose to disclose your situation to others, and addresses your thoughts and feelings around who is or who is not safe to tell. It will help you explore whom you consider to be safe in telling, your motivation for sharing, and the long-term ramifications. It offers suggestions for how to handle those people who may be pushing you for information when it doesn't feel safe or right to do so.*

A consideration that weighs heavily as the shock of the addiction settles in is deciding whether and to whom you should confide. Some partners immediately reach out to a family member or a close friend. For others, it becomes necessary to tell certain people because of immediate decisions that may be made such as the addict or the partner leaving the home. In other cases, the possibility of illicit behaviors resulting in public exposure forces the issue so that you have to tell those people with whom you wouldn't otherwise share such intimate details of your life.

The type of person you are will determine your comfort level in confiding in someone about the addiction. Often messages you tell yourself play a role in whether it is safe to tell others. For example, if you were taught growing up that feelings didn't matter and trusting others leaves you vulnerable, it will be harder for you to open up to others. Confiding about personal problems, especially one as stigmatizing as sex addiction, may make you feel weak and out of control since you'll have to let your guard down, something that is threatening for you. Some partners find that talking through an issue is how they process and make meaning out of their circumstances. It's more an impulse for them to tell others, almost to a fault, as they are at risk of saying too much and isolating themselves from the support they so desperately want.

Whatever your style is, it is important to honor your own comfort. Yet whenever a crisis of this magnitude occurs, further pain and isolation can make an already difficult situation much worse. Talking about what has happened is healing. It is the bridge between the addictive system of lies and secrets and the road to recovery. By letting others in you reduce the shame and stigma surrounding the behaviors of your partner and you glean the wisdom of others, which opens you up to new choices and possible solutions to your problems. This is true for all situations you confront in life. You need people, and as a human being you derive a sense of connection by being in a relationship. Also, by not talking to others you face the risk of becoming anxious or depressed when those emotions are denied and/or pushed aside.

## CONSIDERATIONS WHEN THINKING ABOUT WHOM TO TELL

This exercise presents some guidelines to explore when considering how to tell people about the crisis confronting you.

### Safe People

Identify those people in your life you are considering talking to and then answer the following questions.

- Whom do you consider to be the people you may want to talk to? Who would be both supportive and safe? Supportive people are friends, family members, mentors, spiritual leaders, doctors, and therapists with whom sharing intimate details feels safe to you. These are people whom you trust and whose responses are empathic. What further makes them safe is that their overarching concern is for you and they can respect your need for confidence.

### Motivation

What is your motivation in telling this person? Is it to garner support or is it to get even? Is it to no longer feel the isolation of holding the secrets?

**Long-term Ramifications**

Three months from now, a year from now, or five years from now, will you still feel okay about having shared these intimate details of your life with this person? Some people are very safe in the present moment, but the relationship could change in the future and then they would no longer be a part of your intimate safe circle. For example, you might share with a coworker whom you are fond of, but if in time this coworker becomes your boss, then having your boss know your situation might become uncomfortable. Or sometimes, sharing can strengthen a connection to someone you previously had not considered available enough to shoulder some of your burden.

• Write down any fears you may have about whom to tell.

## TRAFFIC LIGHT ANALOGY

One way to think about who it is you would use or not use for support is the symbol of a traffic light. Those in the *green light* region will be supportive, safe, and trustworthy. What you share with them will be more open and intimate. Then there are those with whom you would like to share but have reasons to be reticent. The *yellow light* area includes those people whom you wouldn't necessarily turn to for emotional support, but would need to inform them for other logistical reasons. Say you and your partner have decided to separate and it is necessary to tell certain friends and family, or at certain events you have contact with someone who asks you why your partner is not with you. These are yellow areas where you wouldn't confide in them, yet you need to reveal enough information to give the impression that the status of the relationship has changed. This helps to keep you on surer footing as you navigate discretion without the fear you'll say too little or nothing at all.

### EXAMPLE

*I wanted you to know that Mary and I have separated. This is a very painful time, but I wanted you to hear it from me rather than someone else.*

Those whom you know will not be supportive belong in the *red light* zone. These people may be the closest to you, like a sister or a parent, but they may be people you know would judge you unfairly or not be empathetic to your plight. Their reactions to your situation would be unhelpful, and in fact, hurtful to you. They may say comments such as, "Leave him." "All men cheat." "How could you stay?" Or they condone or minimize the behavior and imply you are the cause of it. It may be out of ignorance, or possibly these individuals have unresolved issues that make them unavailable to share your concerns. Whatever the case, these are people with whom revealing very little will protect you from emotional harm.

As you think of people in your life, you need to consider: 1) whether or not they can be supportive; 2) if they can keep a confidence safe; 3) your motive; and 4) long-term ramifications.

### EXAMPLES

1. *I have this relatively new friend and we talk every day and I would like to tell her, but her boyfriend works at the same place as my husband and it would not be good if he was aware that I told about our situation.*

   **Support**: *Yes*　　　**Safe**: *No*　　　**Motive**: *Positive*　　　**Ramifications**: *Questionable*

2. *I would like to talk to my boss because at times we have talked personally, but politics can change at work and this may not be the best situation.*

   **Support**: *Yes*　　**Safe**: *Questionable*　　**Motive**: *Positive*　　**Ramifications**: *Questionable*

3. *I want to tell my mom because if I don't, someone else will and there's no telling what she'll be told. She will be so angry with my husband, she'll feel compelled to tell her friends and very likely create stress for me by becoming preoccupied with my situation.*

   **Support**: *Questionable*　　　**Safe**: *Questionable*　　　**Motive**: *Positive*
   **Ramifications**: *Questionable*

4. *I want to tell my sister-in-law. She is forever telling me how lucky I am to be married to such a good provider and she needs to know what a skunk my husband really is.*

   **Support**: *No*　　**Safe**: *Questionable*　　**Motive**: *Negative*　　**Ramifications**: *Questionable*

5. *I want to tell my friend Susie because she is trustworthy and will be of great support to me.*

   **Support**: *Yes*　　**Safe**: *Yes*　　**Motive**: *Positive*　　**Ramifications**: *None*

6. *I want to tell my sister Dee because she will be caring and supportive and allow me to tell others when I'm ready.*

**Support**: *Yes*  **Safe**: *Yes*  **Motive**: *Positive*  **Ramifications**: *None*

Some people, such as examples five and six, will be very clear options for you. They will be supportive, safe, and trustworthy. Consider them green light people. Those who are not safe, trustworthy, or supportive, such as example four, are red light people. Then there are those with whom you would like to share, but have reasons to be reticent. Those are yellow light people, such as examples one, two, and three.

Using the following graphic as a guide, identify the people in your life who you will or will not tell and place them in the corresponding color that best fits.

**EXAMPLES**

**<u>Green Light</u>** *(those whom I choose to tell freely)*
*Susie*
*Sister Dee*

**<u>Yellow Light</u>** *(those whom I choose to tell with discretion)*
*mother*
*boss*
*new friend*

**<u>Red Light</u>** *(those to whom it is unsafe to say anything)*
*sister-in-law*

## SCRIPTING CHALLENGING CONVERSATIONS

Take time to consider situations where you might be asked questions about your relationship, particularly with those people you've put in your yellow or red light categories. Tailoring your story protects your privacy and aids you in not saying more than intended. In these types of situations, you might address the essentials of the crisis, but leave out your emotion or judgment. Typically, you'll want to limit what you say by structuring it into three to four sentences.

An example of a response to someone who has heard there was a divorce or separation might be: *"I am not comfortable sharing details, but yes, Mary and I are separated. Thank you for your concern."* The "thank you for concern" conveys that you are finished talking about this.

Or when he or she asks where your partner is: *"Mary is not able to be here tonight, but I am glad to be here."* The statement acknowledges the comment and redirects the focus to you and away from your absent partner. By making a statement, you are not openly inviting dialogue and instead are conveying a shift in the conversation.

Sometimes, people will be more aggressive in wanting to know your business. Unfortunately this can be challenging and may be more indicative about them. *"Oh my gosh Susan, I just heard these rumors about Kevin, what is going on?"* You respond with a fact that offers little detail and with a tone to close the questioning. *"This is a very difficult time. I hope you can respect our need for privacy."*

If the person continues to press with: *"But I feel so bad for you."* Wait as if you will now share more detail, and say: *"As I said, this is a really difficult time; there are problems, and I hope you will respect our need for privacy."*

Considering the above suggestions, if there are yellow or red light people who you anticipate talking to, take this time to write out what you might say. Share only what you are comfortable sharing. What you share with people needs to be determined according to 1) support, 2) safety, 3) motive, and 4) the possible ramifications.

It is helpful if you and your partner are in agreement as to who will or will not be told. For a variety of reasons this does not always work out. There may be people who you feel are important enough to tell, but whom your partner may not. Although this presents a conflict between the two of you, if your motivation is for you and supports you in your healing, then acting on your own behalf becomes part of your healing journey. In these instances, having some agreement as to what gets disclosed is where common ground can be made between you and your partner. While situations vary, it is respectful to tell your partner with whom it is you are sharing.

Knowing your motivation will help to direct you in determining with whom you will share and to what depth of detail you will share. You want to honor yourself and no longer engage in behaviors that keep you in a victim role or that isolate you in such a manner that causes your pain to escalate. At the same time you need to give consideration to those who are most safe. You will find in time the answer to this question becomes clear.

## Developing a Strong Support System

*The need for support that goes beyond family and friends is addressed in the following section. Several possibilities to meet those needs are presented, as well as useful resources. You also will be guided through exercises that help you explore those self-sabotaging beliefs that hinder your efforts to reach out and allow others to be there for you. You will then identify new beliefs that may help you to incorporate additional support.*

Seeking support means reaching out for help where and when you can. It can bridge the distance between living with despair and shame versus living with self-respect and dignity. In the previous exercise "Deciding Whom to Tell," you explored those relationships closest to you and thought through who was or was not safe to tell about the immediate crisis. Some of these people are friends and family, some are not. Beginning to let others know what you're going through is a big step in breaking the isolation you are feeling. Finding a good support system is another such step in the healing process, as it is more focused on finding specialized help pertaining to the crisis at hand.

Part of living in an addictive system is the social and emotional isolation that can occur over time. This is particularly true when the nature of the problem is sexual addiction. It can be very scary to ask for help. You may find it difficult to let your guard down and allow others to help you. Even if you want support, you may not know how to find it.

Regardless of the type of person you are, outgoing or reserved, cautious or too-trusting, asking for help may bring up negative messages about whether you will get what you need or if you deserve it. Often these messages originate from your family and the environment in which you were raised. Many partners describe homes where they felt alone in coping with problems. Many may not even remember asking for help. Many grew up in families where there was addiction and the secrets and shame that supported the maladaptive behaviors meant it was not okay to let others outside the family know its problems.

These types of scenarios result in an emotionally invalidating environment and affect how you relate to others in adult relationships. You learned that asking for help backfired and that rigid self-reliance was the best way to survive and adapt in your family. How you thought about your circumstances helped you tolerate a system in which you were meant to serve the needs of the family, not the other way around.

Today you may recognize your self-talk as a hindrance to getting the support you need. You fear that no one will really understand and they will judge you. Your thoughts become a self-sabotaging cycle of beliefs that hinder your efforts to get better.

Let's first look at roadblocks to seeking support. What do you tell yourself that prevents you from reaching out and allowing others to help you? In your journal, write those statements from the list below that you most identify with.

- No one really cares about my problems.
- Everyone has their own problems; I don't need to burden them with mine.
- They won't understand the issue and will only want to blame me.
- They will tell me to leave him or her.
- It's wrong to lean on others. I should be able to handle this myself.
- I'm afraid I will need too much and push others away.
- I feel everyone I tell should be there for me all the time.
- This is too humiliating. I will simply fall apart.
- Other thoughts.

- If you do not seek outside support, what will you gain? Will you feel better, worse, or the same? Or, if you do not seek outside support, what will the cost be to you?

- What could you tell yourself that will make it more likely for you to reach out? What are some reasons to reach out for help?

**EXAMPLES**

*I am not the only one who has had to face this.*

.  .  .  .

*It would be nice to meet others in similar situations.*

.  .  .  .

*I don't need to feel ashamed. It will feel good to not be so alone with my thoughts and feelings.*

.  .  .  .

*Others will understand.*

.  .  .  .

*It's okay to ask for help.*

.  .  .  .

*He/she really does care about me and would want to be available to me.*

One of the ways to build a strong support system is to have a therapist. It's important to choose one carefully. Good help feels good, bad help feels confusing or can often make you feel invalidated. Seeking a good therapist can be difficult, especially if you've had experiences with therapists who were ignorant of addiction and ended up worsening the problem, causing you to distrust that any therapist will understand your situation, or that somehow you were to blame for the problems in the relationship. This is especially common when partners have gone for help with couples' therapists who were not trained in treating sex addiction. In these instances, partners reported being made to accept, and in fact, join in aspects of the addict's behavior as a means for increasing intimacy. Far more common is the impression that each partner shares equal responsibility for the problems in the relationship, thereby diluting the obvious damage addictive behavior is doing to the couple. This resulted in partners having their voices invalidated since their concerns ran counter to a traditional couples' therapy model in which problems are viewed as fifty/fifty.

Active sex addiction, whether recognized or not, is like a smoldering fire spreading throughout the home. Sometimes you are the only one saying, "Hey, I think I smell smoke in here. Do you?" only to find that your partner disagrees. Eventually, an uncontained fire burns out of control and outside help is needed. When a couple has a relationship crisis, they often turn to therapy. A trained sex addiction therapist can make all the difference in partners being heard, whereas an untrained therapist may worsen the problem through misdiagnosis or a lack of skills specific to those impacted by sex addiction. This can further damage the couple's relationship, possibly reenacting for a partner the pattern of his or her concerns being invalidated. To ensure that you find help that will be most effective in addressing problematic sexual behaviors you can contact the professional organizations of IITAP (International Institute for Trauma and Addiction Professionals) and SASH (Society for the Advancement of Sexual Health). See the Resources section on page 233.

A way to consider your options for finding help related to sex addiction is to consider where others have gone for help with similar problems. Ways partners have sought outside resources include:

- Therapists: Trained CSAT (Certified Sex Addiction Therapist) or addiction/trauma therapist. Individual therapy—talking to a professional one-on-one. Group therapy—therapist-led group of partners of sex addicts.

- Self-help groups: Peer led—no cost. S-ANON, CO-SLAA, AL-ANON. See Resources.

- Self-help books.

- Internet: Websites and chat rooms for recovery discussion and information.

- Residential treatment: For addiction, trauma, and psychiatric disorders.

- Outpatient programs: For addiction, trauma, and psychiatric disorders.

- Workshops/Intensives: Typically five to ten days to focus on particular trauma-related themes that are best addressed in a more structured setting.

- Religious groups or organizations.

- Retreats—religious or meditative.

- Legal advice.

- Job training: To offer you more choices.

- Domestic violence counseling.

Recognizing and incorporating support into your daily life will make a huge difference in how you weather the changes ahead. Be aware that support needs can change as people can change. Try not to put all your needs for help into one basket. Diversify and recognize the limits and benefits of each resource. By following this suggestion, you will become more aware of how your needs can be met in different ways under different circumstances.

You do not deserve to live with the emotional or social isolation that comes with sexual shame and secrets, and by reaching out for support you work to overcome those risks. Seeking support is a sign of strength. It means you can hear and be heard; you can see and be seen. Support will make life more stable.

## The Road Ahead

*You have done a lot of work up to this point, and we hope you are beginning to feel less crisis-driven, more grounded, and more stable. Some of you may have welcomed putting pen to paper. At times, it may have been difficult to see your reality written down, but being able to express your experiences to the degree you felt capable likely offered some relief. Some of you may have struggled and had to push through resistance, maybe still expecting immediate answers. For now, please accept our congratulations for doing the work you have done thus far. It's important work. You are setting the foundation for your recovery.*

# CHAPTER TWO

# *Turning Inward*

This is a time of incredible grief and uncertainty, where the road ahead is unclear. Being in a relationship with a sex addict means you have been in a chronic state of loss, perhaps for a long time. With your grief process, there are a multitude of feelings that usually become dismissed or distorted. In this process, it is likely you have lost sight of your personal strengths. The areas explored in this chapter are intended to offer you a greater foundation to continue your recovery. The exercises provide a framework to better understand what is happening emotionally to you and ways in which to cope.

# Vision for Self

*Here you will have the opportunity to assess what you have to gain by investing in yourself and your healing process. The exercises help you to recognize that there are many fears to this healing process and will walk you through acknowledging those fears while focusing on your self-care. Confronting your fears and deepening your commitment moves you out of the problem toward the solution.*

Aside from the consuming worries and fears about your partner's recovery or the relationship's survival, it may be difficult to even muster the strength to look ahead. The idea of delving deeper into what this betrayal means to you may seem scary since it will dredge up so much pain. You may feel as though you're going backward, or your experience of discovery may have you feeling relieved because you realize what you need to do to be able to move forward.

Part of being an unwitting partner to someone else's sex addiction is the victimization that results from being deceived. Being victimized is a result of someone else's power over you, and it affects many areas of your life, especially your choices about having a voice in your relationship. Partners of sex addicts, whether they know of the addiction or not, often spend a lot of time allowing their views of themselves and the addict to be molded and shaped according to the addict's beliefs. This can be subtle, overt, or both and it doesn't necessarily permeate every aspect of who you are, but occurs in those core areas where love, companionship, and support most matter, eroding your self-respect in the process.

Overcoming victimization takes time and considerable investment in yourself. Recognizing your choices, asking for help, and gathering the wisdom of others are all steps that move you out of entrapment and toward freedom and choice. Creating a vision for yourself in this way means exploring how you were trapped, coerced, or manipulated, or codependently tolerated more than was appropriate. Recognizing that these relational patterns existed and changing course allows you to be better equipped to handle the road ahead. But it begins with you and assessing what you have to gain by investing in yourself.

Women and men who have taken this journey found it allowed them to trust their intuition and recognize choices. Many found themselves no longer depressed or anxious. They came to know the difference between being manipulated and knowing what they truly wanted for themselves. Many said they could laugh again and were more confident or were able to be a more present parent. Creating meaning out of your suffering and shaping a vision of your future can offer you new possibilities.

This exercise is an opportunity to consider the gifts of continuing to move your journey forward.

- What is your vision of what you would like to gain for yourself in working through this crisis?

- Do you have any fears about what would or would not happen if you pursued this vision? How realistic is each fear?

- Is there anyone with whom you could discuss how realistic these fears are?

- Even if the fears played out in some way, could the good outweigh the bad? If so, what would be the good that could outweigh the bad?

- While holding your vision of the good and acknowledging any fears, describe an image, feeling, or sensation in your body that best represents that positive vision.

For the following exercises, you'll need to create three columns in your journal with these headers: **Gained**; **Remain the Same**; and **Lost**.

- If you **pursue this vision,** what would be gained, remain the same, or be lost?

- If you **don't pursue this vision,** what would be gained, remain the same, or be lost?

You have been living in the shadow of someone else's behavior. As you step outside of that shadow, it becomes easier to see the possibilities for yourself and to feel the hope that can be there. As you take each step in the recovery process, your vision for self will become more clear and inviting.

# Living in Limbo

*Here we will help you acknowledge that as you move from the immediate crisis, you enter an in-between state of not knowing where the relationship is going, where you want it to go, or even how it will get there. The fears you have about whether your addicted partner can stay open, honest, and in recovery only increase your uncertainty. While this state cannot be bypassed, it can be tolerated. The exercises allow you to describe this experience and to recognize the gifts that can come if you don't resist.*

Although the immediate crisis may have receded and you're at a stage where the pain, although not far away, has quieted a bit, the emotional toll of the sexual betrayal is immense. It is as if you are living a bad dream or a Greek tragedy that has no ending. Your naïveté or lost innocence and the shattering of all your dreams confront you on a daily basis. Most damaging is the contamination of your basic trust in human beings. All relationships are now potentially suspect and you find yourself in a new place—one for which there is no map to follow.

Sometimes shifting from the acute phase of worrying and reactivity to a lull in managing the crisis shows up in how you feel emotionally. One woman found, after months of being in a hypervigilant state, she couldn't get out of bed in the morning. Another described the tears that came every night as she was getting ready for bed. Before she had only felt anger at her husband for cheating, but now she cries herself to sleep every night.

### EXAMPLES
*I remember walking around for weeks as if in a daze. I can't even remember details of my life when I think back to that time. Now is different. I awake in the middle of the night and my heart feels heavy. I can't get back to sleep for several hours, but I know it's the pain of what I'm going through.*

· · · ·

*I've lived with chronic forms of abuse from my partner for more than thirty years and learned six months ago that he has been having sex with males and females. I just feel dead from the new onslaught of information. I'm not crying, I'm not even angry, I'm not anything.*

· · · ·

*When I gave up my chronic detective work—checking on whether my husband was doing his program—I had more time for myself. I started to create self-care rituals, such as taking a bath with lighted candles and reading self-help books focusing on affirmations.*

Can you relate to any of these examples? If yes, describe.

Others describe this time as a period of limbo where there are no imminent changes required of them or the relationship. It's more a time of preparedness for the next phase of their healing.

**EXAMPLES**

*I was just waiting to see where the relationship was going to go. I could see my partner was making changes. But I was still nowhere near ready to decide to recommit to the relationship, nor was I ready to leave. What was I waiting for? I just couldn't seem to decide what I wanted to do.*

· · · ·

*The initial fears had subsided. I was no longer bracing for a new secret or discovery of his acting out. I was not searching through his things. But I was impatient with myself; I didn't know what was next. It seemed like the calm after the storm, but was there another one coming? I didn't know; it seemed as though things were changing, but I couldn't see where I was headed. I had already decided to separate but I couldn't act upon the decision. I felt stuck, yet my therapist told me that this is part of living in limbo. I was finished doing the same things in the relationship, but I didn't yet have a new way to behave. I felt lost.*

• What does it mean to you to live in limbo?

• Where do you feel you should be versus where you are?

• What is holding you back from making changes?

Partners often live in a state of chaos or unpredictability. Conversely, some partners are so trusting that they avoid feelings that would generate unease or suspicion, choosing instead to have blind faith in the addict. Both ways serve as a distraction from consistently trusting your own reality over the addict's. Therefore, when the acute part of the drama in the relationship quiets—and it will—you are forced to look within and face many feelings that you have avoided. Typically these feelings are ones of grief and loss, anger and sadness. Delving into these feelings becomes essential to your healing and the state of limbo evolves into a personal journey toward greater awareness of who you are in the world around you.

- What would it mean to you right now if there were no immediate action or decision to be made about the relationship?

- If you could project a year from now, what would you like to be different about you, the relationship, and the addict?

- What is the worst part of being where you are right now? What is the best part?

- What could you do to make this time more nurturing to you? This could be things such as sitting quietly and having a cup a tea, taking time out for exercise or relaxation, attending a twelve-step meeting, or calling a friend.

Hopefully, by now, living in the in-between state is more tolerable and not so frightening. This is a natural state and one that is necessary as you move forward.

## Defining Trauma Responses

*Now we will take you through a process where you will explore responses to experiencing trauma. You will be able to identify whether or not you are experiencing signs of post-traumatic stress disorder and the common symptoms that relate to partners of sex addicts. You'll explore the various degrees of victimization as you gain clarity about the manner in which you were victimized. Reflecting on the degree of victimization and/or trauma you have experienced will help define your commitment to recovery. It concludes by supporting you in creating safety as you continue along your healing journey.*

Now that you have identified your losses as a result of disclosure/discovery, it is important to acknowledge how you've been victimized. When we think of being a victim, we think of someone helpless, overpowered, and trapped. Those words in fact may describe how you are feeling or felt when you learned the truth. Your partner's behavior has been traumatic and has caused you injury, and recovering from this damage is imperative. You were helpless over what he or she did and feel powerless to change it. But coming to terms with this victimization means rebounding and claiming power and responsibility for what is in your control going forward and making choices about what you will and will not accept in the relationship.

Typical reactions in someone who has been violated are symptoms commonly found with post-traumatic stress disorder (PTSD). Post-traumatic stress disorder simply put means "after-trauma-anxiety-reaction." It consists of a cluster of symptoms, which characterize emotional problems that occur for greater than a month following a life-threatening, horrific event. Your experience of learning about your spouse's/partner's addiction is an example of this.

Below are symptoms of PSTD. Write down all of the symptoms that apply to see if PSTD fits for you:

- **Intrusion:** You find your mind can't stop thinking about the problem. This can occur in the form of intrusive images, nightmares, or flashbacks.

- **Avoidance:** Numbing, feeling detached, avoiding any reminders of the event.

- **Arousal:** Feeling on guard; hyperaroused. Easily startled and triggered by situations that remind you of the crisis.

- **Lower functioning:** Not able to perform at usual level with work, relationships, or other major areas of your life.

PTSD can be characterized as a single event, such as a car accident, or a series of events over a long period of time, like childhood abuse or repeated hospitalizations for a medical condition. There are basic and complex symptoms common to both forms of PTSD and broader ones that encompass more symptoms. Similarly, some partners either knew a problem existed and had poor coping skills to confront it, or were completely in the dark and were blindsided by the deception.

Following are typical symptoms found with those having PTSD as it pertains to partners of sex addicts. Write down those with which you identify:

- Betrayal of trust: Fear of trusting the addict and yourself.

- Psychic and physical pain and anguish: Range of emotions that at times feel out of control. Increased headaches, back, and neck aches, stomach problems.

- Hypervigilance: Fear that the other shoe is going to drop.

- Preoccupation: Obsessing about the addiction and worrying about whether to stay or leave the relationship.

- Loss of safety and security: Sexual, financial, and emotional fears grow and/or increase.

Other ways the trauma has affected you involve how you perceive yourself and others. Review the list below and write down those which most apply to you.

- I fear men/women.

- I fear sex.

- I don't know what to believe.

- I am sad a great deal of the time.

- I can't focus on my kids or my job.

- I feel I walk around in a cloud all day.

- I fear for the future because everything about the relationship feels uncertain.

- I want answers, and I am filled with insecurity, causing me to look at my partner's email accounts or check on his or her whereabouts.

PTSD symptoms and triggers are reenacted as a result of the crisis before you. Some of you will find that you recover more quickly than others who find the pain takes longer to move through. Be patient.

## VICTIMIZATION

You will find that the degree of victimization is greater or less depending on how long you knew a problem existed, but did not confront it. This is comparable to driving a car and failing to use the turn signal with the result that the driver behind you rear-ends your car—you would share some responsibility.

- **Victimization with minor guilt**: *Knew he was flirting with other women and did nothing about it.*

- **Victimization with equal responsibility**: *Agreed to sexual acts that involved others believing she needed this type of release.*

- **Victimization with greater responsibility**: *After all the ways he hurt me, I wanted to get back at him so I had his girlfriend followed and told her employer. I also told our kids so they'd be against him.*

- **Victimization with total responsibility**: *I ran over her laptop and broke the window on her car, and she pressed charges against me.*

Various levels of victimization: where are you on the continuum?

Knew nothing                                                              Knew a lot

0 ———————————————— 50 ———————————————— 100

- Can you relate to any of the four types of victimization and if so, explain?

- Write a short synopsis of how you were victimized by the addiction.

## WHAT DO I DO NOW?

Challenging life situations happen to all of us, but it is the coping skills applied that distinguish those who fare better. The path ahead of you means turning your

- Helplessness to accountability;

- Hopelessness to empowerment; and

- Blame to responsibility.

Reflecting on the degree of victimization and trauma you where exposed to gives you an opportunity to consider the commitment you're prepared to make to end your suffering that has been created by the addiction.

Contract to myself: As a commitment to end my victimization, I make the following pledge:

EXAMPLES

*End my denial at all costs.*

.  .  .  .

*Stay in recovery group.*

.  .  .  .

*Stop making excuses for my partner or myself.*

If I fail to follow through with my commitments I understand that I will lose . . .

## SAFETY

When you experience trauma, you may find your emotions and behaviors become unpredictable. Your world feels uncertain and chaotic. Further, you are being bombarded with a lot of new information you never imagined being exposed to, such as explicit details of sexual behavior, the language of recovery, possible legal data, treatment protocol, etc. Paying attention when life is out of control necessitates being patient with your feelings, as behavior and thoughts are going to be in upheaval.

The biggest concern for most people who experience victimization is safety. It can come in various forms, and it is the first priority. It means gaining control over your feelings, learning to cope with day-to-day issues, and protecting yourself from hurtful people and situations. It means being gentle with yourself, building healthy relationships with others, and not engaging in self-harming behaviors.

## AREAS WHERE SELF-PROTECTION IS NEEDED

EXAMPLES

**Physical and Emotional**: *Removing myself from situations where I fear my safety is in jeopardy.*

**Reality Testing**: *Inviting those closest to me whom I trust to be honest with me regarding decisions I am considering, even if the truth hurts.*

**Emotion Regulation**: *Becoming able to identify when my emotions are on overdrive and using self-soothing techniques to calm myself and/or deep breathing and meditation to bring some detachment to the situations that trigger me.*

By owning your victimization, you give voice to how you've been exploited and duped by your loved one's lies and half-truths. Recognizing the implications of the addictive behavior offers you a way out of the pain and a path toward a new beginning based on truth and self-respect. We applaud you for the courage it takes to look at this painful reality and again encourage you to open yourself to the various means available to soothe and nurture your growth.

## Grieving the Betrayals

*We will now describe the grief process that occurs with the many losses resulting from living with sexual deception—losses within the relationship, the loss of your self-confidence, your hopes and dreams. You will gain a better understanding of common roadblocks to the grief process and the tools to circumvent them. By validating and normalizing your grief process you become more accepting of yourself.*

Although no one has died, the relationship as you knew it has. You question the past and whether moments of intimacy with your partner were real or part of the deception. Your self-confidence and the innocence you once had are shaken. The dreams for the future are shattered as it is difficult to imagine a tomorrow with your spouse or partner. From this place it is difficult to trust him or her, yourself, or anyone else since you believe your intuition is no longer reliable. With what you now know, you find yourself filtering the relationship through the lens of deceptions, half-truths, and blatant lies. All of these experiences have catapulted you into a grief process that if left unexplored, can have a negative effect on your health and well-being.

The classic grief model is one proposed by Elizabeth Kübler-Ross in her groundbreaking work with the dying. It asserts that there is a universal process to grieving with predictable stages people move through as they contend with the loss, eventually leading to a resolution. Her model was initially intended for those facing death and later became adapted to various forms of illness and losses people confront throughout the life cycle. It is one we think you will find helpful.

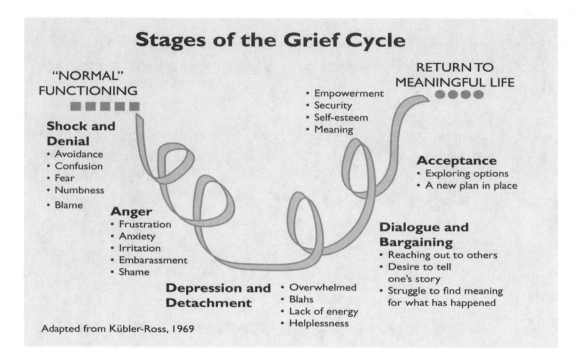

**Stages of the Grief Cycle**

"NORMAL" FUNCTIONING

**Shock and Denial**
• Avoidance
• Confusion
• Fear
• Numbness
• Blame

**Anger**
• Frustration
• Anxiety
• Irritation
• Embarassment
• Shame

**Depression and Detachment**
• Overwhelmed
• Blahs
• Lack of energy
• Helplessness

RETURN TO MEANINGFUL LIFE

• Empowerment
• Security
• Self-esteem
• Meaning

**Acceptance**
• Exploring options
• A new plan in place

**Dialogue and Bargaining**
• Reaching out to others
• Desire to tell one's story
• Struggle to find meaning for what has happened

Adapted from Kübler-Ross, 1969

The losses you are experiencing are multifaceted and often chronic in nature for they involve not only the loss of a partner, as you knew him or her, but also the loss of yourself. Your grieving process is uniquely your own and will progress at a pace that is right for you. Timing, prior losses, and the degree of complexity of your situation, as well as your own constitution will play a role in how you move through these stages.

In learning about these stages, it is important to interpret them loosely and to expect that there will be a variation based on your unique circumstances. There is no neat or linear progression from one stage to the next, as grief is not one-dimensional but rather a jumble of many different feelings. You may also find that you stay in some stages longer than others. Expect that there will be times when you loop back to an earlier stage as you progress in your healing. Our experience has shown us that those willing to stay with the healing process do get to a place of acceptance and gain the ability to move forward.

## SHOCK AND DENIAL

When the reality of what was happening became apparent, you may have reacted in numb disbelief. The shock that your partner had been cheating for so long and the understandable refusal to accept what was occurring are ways the mind contended with the trauma. "This can't be!" "I can't believe she would go online and meet men!" "There is no way he was viewing illegal porn. The police have the wrong person." When truth is so painful and overwhelming, denial, minimization, and rationalization are spontaneous responses that initially serve to protect you from the reality of what is occurring. You may find yourself blaming someone else for the trauma and initially feel joined with your partner. You may be blaming the police for their rough treatment of your partner; blaming your partner's parents for raising him or her the way they did; blaming the pornography industry; or the affair partner for cheating when he or she knew the addict was committed to someone else. These types of reactions serve to insulate you from the full truth. This stage can last from a few weeks to months.

Describe three examples that demonstrated you were in shock and denial after discovery/disclosure.

## ANGER

Anger is a natural response to a loss. It is a protest—a declaration that what is happening is wrong and unjust. When you have been mistreated and taken advantage of, anger is a healthy reaction. It heightens your awareness, readies you for self-protection, and propels you toward action. Without it you lack the courage to speak out, to seek justice, or to protect yourself from further harm. Some partners felt so outraged during their grief that they immediately asked the addict to move out. Others took off their wedding rings or removed all pictures of them as a couple. Others' grief response was to hold firm to treatment expectations and bottom lines they'd established and expected of the addict in the first year. And still some partners felt their minds awash in thoughts of anger directed at the addict, the sex industry, or God.

Give three examples of how you experienced anger as a grief response.

If over time your anger becomes the go-to emotion and you find yourself feeling hostile and blaming most of the time, this is a sign that you are misdirecting your anger. You find anger is more comfortable because it gives you a greater sense of self-control, as it defends you from emotions that elicit vulnerability. Some partners fear being vulnerable because it brings them back to the time of the discovery/disclosure again. By dealing directly with your anger you validate and clarify the unfairness of the loss and allow other emotions and phases of the grief process to emerge.

Or you may find that you avoid anger. When you fear rejection, are afraid of the reality, and/or are highly dependent on your partner's approval, you may have difficulty owning your anger. You don't want to be angry, and you relate more to stages of depression or sorrow. When this stage in the grieving process is bypassed and avoided, you jeopardize learning how to self-protect. To not feel indignant over what your partner did affects your ability to draw a line and say enough is enough. Anger is essential if you are to move from victimization toward empowerment.

Give three examples of situations when you had cause to be angry and were unable to experience or express anger.

Ultimately, the goal is to be able to acknowledge your anger, work with it, and find useful ways to move through the emotion.

## BARGAINING

As painful as it is for anyone to wend their way through a grief process, many people find a type of psychological safety in bargaining. You get caught up in all the possibilities that could have been averted to prevent the outcome, and it serves as a distraction from what has happened and also as a means to come to grips with what is going on.

This is likely when you are thinking out loud or seeking others' support, and you might ask those larger questions such as: What was he thinking? Why is this so painful? Will she ever get better? Will I ever feel better? When does the pain end? Bargaining is often an internal dialogue with your higher power or yourself. Prayers such as, "Dear God, I promise to be a better wife if you would just keep him faithful." Or, "I promise to go to church and serve you more if you just keep her from having any slips," provide a sense of control over the outcome of the crisis facing you. It is also manifested in your relationship with the addict. "I told him I would engage in different types of sexual behavior if he promised to stop looking at porn at night." "If she flirts with her colleague again, I'm kicking her out." "Only if something worse happens will I . . ."

Give three examples of how you have engaged in bargaining.

Guilt is a natural response to loss and often accompanies feelings of sadness and bargaining. There is both true and false guilt—*true guilt* is a feeling of regret or remorse over something you have or have not done. *False guilt* is the feeling of regret or remorse for someone else's behavior and actions. If you have difficulty separating true guilt from false guilt, you are likely experiencing complicated grief whereby the loss is fused with other variables besides the addiction. A death in the family or a child with multiple medical problems are examples of loss being fused with other significant life changes. You question whether you did enough and berate yourself for not knowing you were being deceived. You wonder what you could have done to make things different. "If I had paid more attention to him . . ." or "If I did what she wanted sexually . . ." or "If I had been home more . . ." Even if you rationally accept the problem as belonging to your partner, the guilt response is your emotional self coming to grips with what you've lost. You will be free from the carried guilt when you face those feelings of guilt by recognizing where responsibility lies and taking responsibility for what is yours.

Give three examples of guilt, either true or false guilt, that you have experienced.

The bargaining stage can delay facing the reality of your situation by keeping you from addressing the totality of what is happening. To move through this stage of grief means allowing yourself to acknowledge feelings you wish to avoid. Acceptance is often one most betrayed partners struggle to acknowledge. "He is a sex addict." "She has left me for the addiction," are all ways to consciously face the truth. Next, try to find small safe steps that allow you to tolerate and feel the associated feelings linked to the avoided emotion. Writing, meditation and/or prayer, or a ritual behavior such as taking a memento and burning it are ways to acknowledge and make your grief real. Over time as you move forward in recovery, you will develop the ability to tolerate your feelings with less self-defeating or otherwise self-destructive behaviors.

## DEPRESSION

Sorrow is a normal part of the grieving process, and it serves to give meaning to how much the person and situation has meant to you. Feeling sorrow often allows you the space and time necessary to acknowledge and experience the sadness. You have many reasons to be sad. There are multiple losses you confront as a result of the intimate betrayal by your partner. If this crisis fuels dormant and pervasive feelings about your self-worth, expect these insights to heighten during the depression stage of grief. This stage may take more time, especially if the loss is fused with other issues. Sometimes referred to as complicated grief, the stages of grief are compounded by multiple variables such as previous losses and inadequate levels of support. If you believe you aren't worthy or there is no hope, then you can easily succumb to the power of defeat, become depressed, and stay stuck in the grief process.

Give three examples of times when you experienced overwhelming sorrow.

## ACCEPTANCE

It is unlikely, at this stage of working the exercises in this book that you have come to a place of acceptance of all that you have lost. The goals for now are to 1) Recognize that you are in a grief process and allow self-compassion for all that you are feeling; and 2) Recognize and gather support to mobilize yourself if there is an area in this process in which you have a tendency to become stuck. Acceptance comes as a result of being able to experience each step of the grief process. Acceptance does not mean that what he or she has done is okay or is not hurtful. It means accepting the reality of his or her behavior and its impact on you, your relationship, and your family. Finding meaning for yourself from this experience is significant in your healing process. You are moving into acceptance with your willingness to explore your options, engage in recovery practices, and make choices that empower and strengthen your self-respect and integrity.

Give three examples that demonstrate your acceptance about your circumstances today. If you don't think you are experiencing acceptance in any area, give examples of actions you are taking that assist you in getting to a place of greater acceptance.

- Review the dynamics of loss and grief—shock and denial, anger, bargaining, depression, and acceptance. Describe what your grief process looks like and identify the area(s) where you have a tendency to become stuck.

- What beliefs and behaviors interfere with your ability to move through the grief process?

In times of intense feelings, you need to take deliberate steps to lessen your external stresses, so this is not the time to take on added responsibilities. Don't put expectations or "shoulds" on yourself. Be aware that the stages of grief invite you to become more vulnerable with yourself so that self-care is very important. Pay special attention to how you handle tasks of daily living. Eating healthily, exercising, resting, and utilizing your support system are decisions you can make to treat yourself gently and with kindness. Getting through the grief process takes time. People who actively engage in their recovery find that the pain gradually diminishes. With the help of others in recovery and/or a professional, you'll find you're able to work through your grief in your own time.

## My Losses

*In this section, we will guide you in exploring the innumerable losses you are experiencing. You will identify general areas of loss and highlight those specific incidents or situations that speak to your personal pain. It is these losses that represent your grief. As you identify your losses you take the first step in letting go of denial about how you have been affected by the betrayal.*

When you learned that you'd been lied to, you were catapulted into an unwelcome reality. The relationship as you knew it changed as your memories became contaminated by what you'd learned. Your dating and courtship, vacations, shared friendships, birth of children, times alone, and goals and dreams became filtered through the framework of addiction, and with that a barrage of conflicting feelings about your shared history together. As you try to make sense of the lies and half-truths, the past seems like a sham. You question your memories of the past: "Was he or she acting out then?" "What can I believe?" The implicit trust you may have had is now replaced with doubts about your shared history.

Part of recognizing what you're facing is acknowledging the multiple losses confronting you. In the earlier exercise, "The Ripple Effect," you identified areas of your life that are changing as the consequences of your partner's behaviors become realized. In this exercise, you will begin to address those losses more specifically as a way to begin grieving them. Your losses are both tangible and intangible since they involve the internal experience as expressed in your values, self-worth, and perceptions of others, combined with the external realities of the consequences of being in a relationship with a sex addict.

Intangible losses are cumulative. They are noticeable because you now experience yourself and life differently than before. One of the most profound losses is the confidence you felt about your relationship. Instead, you may fear your future because you've lost any clear direction of where or what to envision for yourself or the relationship. The predictability in which you lived feels as though it has been ripped away and replaced with pervasive self-doubt and cynicism. Thoughts like: "All men/women lie and cheat" and "No one is trustworthy" become a part of your thinking.

While some tangible losses are immediate, others seem to creep up on you, and only in retrospect do you notice other ways you were affected. There may be loss of opportunity in the workplace due to diminished functioning on your part, or your work may have been impaired due to needed time off to cope with personal problems. Your partner may have lost his or her job, resulting in your making changes in your work status. While employment losses also contribute to financial losses, other financial costs are the additional monies needed for counseling or treatment, the costs of supporting two households due to separation, or the family budget being diminished by the costs related to the acting-out behavior. Examples of sexual loss may be your health that is put at risk or the lack of sexual enjoyment due to mistrust. Loss related to legal issues may have to do with restricting your social world due to those legal issues, such as the financial loss of hiring attorney(s). Parenting loss is most often about the loss of time as a parent or inability to be more available to your children. These are just a few examples, as the losses are many and varied, and individual to you and your circumstances. Yet, there is no doubt that living with addiction creates incredible loss over time, and it's important to be able to name and acknowledge all the ways that your life has been affected.

Below are examples of the areas in which you may have experienced both intangible and tangible losses. In your journal, list all that apply.

| Intangible losses | Tangible losses |
|---|---|
| Self-confidence | Employment |
| Trust | Financial |
| Innocence | Sexual |
| Relationship as you knew it | Legal |
| Fears | Parenting |
| Dreams for the future | Friends |
| Uncertainty | |
| Cynicism for the future | |
| Negativity about people and relationships | |
| Safety and predictability | |
| Relationship to God or a higher power | |
| Values compromised or altered to meet partner's expectations | |
| Loss of direction | |

- As you went through the list above, memories may have emerged that highlighted your losses. Identify those memories or situations in which you felt loss.

By identifying specific events or circumstances directly caused by the addict's behavior you acknowledge what you've lost. This can further your healing and help you in rebuilding your sense of self, little by little. This is an opportunity meant to give you a chance to validate how being misled has resulted in terrible consequences to you.

**EXAMPLES**

*He cheated with my best friend.*

· · · ·

*He wasn't there when our first child was born.*

· · · ·

*I asked her over and over if she was cheating and she told me no.*

· · · ·

*He told lies and more lies.*

· · · ·

*She slept with our neighbor, my best friend, so I thought.*

· · · ·

*He committed to getting into recovery only to cheat further, resulting in my leaving the relationship.*

· · · ·

*He wasn't there for the kids' activities and I covered for him repeatedly only now realizing he was using the time to go act out.*

· · · ·

*She withheld sex.*

· · · ·

*He made me feel stupid.*

Write a letter to yourself about what you feel you have lost about *you*. Keep it personal by using "I" statements to help stay in the experience.

Dear Self,

I have lost:                                    *I feel about these losses:*

**EXAMPLE**
*Dear Self,*
*When I found out he was cheating I was a stay-at-home mom. We agreed to this in part because we felt it best for our kids, but also so he could advance his career. Now I think I was supporting his addiction by innocently accepting his work schedule,*

*which only demanded more and more of his time. How could I have been so duped? I feel ashamed and angry, and I feel stupid for trusting him. I feel I lost trust. I feel I lost self-confidence.*

Identifying, experiencing, and grieving your losses can help move you toward acceptance of this crisis. But to do this you need time and space to reflect on how various parts of your life have been affected by the addiction. Recognizing the lies, distortions, criticisms, contradictions, living in extremes, and chronic half-truths that have come to dominate your relationship will set you on a course to free you from the responsibility of your partner's addiction and help you work to clarify what you are grieving, ultimately setting you on a course toward acceptance and change.

## Letters to Myself

*Now we will help you move further through the grief process and at the same time learn to reclaim your needs and wants. It's an opportunity to be clear about the losses while being empathetic to yourself. The exercises are in the form of letter writing, such as "My Goodbye Letter to My Relationship as It Once Was"; "My Letter about How I Want to be Treated"; and "My Letter of Self-Forgiveness." These letters will affirm your commitment to you.*

One of the greatest losses you are experiencing is the loss of the relationship as you knew it. Even if the relationship was not always strong and healthy, there was likely greater cohesion, a sense of safety, trust, and fun prior to the crisis where you came to recognize the pervasiveness of the acting-out behaviors. You've lost the optimism you had about your future, and your beliefs that people close to you are trustworthy. With loss there is grief, and the healing of that grief begins with recognizing the reality of what you've lost.

In this exercise you have an opportunity to explore how the addictive behaviors progressively impacted the relationship. Acknowledgment furthers your healing, readying you in making future decisions about your life. These are letters you will write to yourself as if you are talking to a dear friend, but you will not give these letters to anyone. In the first letter, you will describe how your relationship, as you once knew it, has changed. In the second letter, you have the opportunity to explore how you'd want to be treated in this or future relationships, and the last letter offers the opportunity for self-forgiveness.

# MY GOODBYE LETTER TO MY RELATIONSHIP AS IT ONCE WAS

Write a letter to yourself, describing how your relationship changed as a result of the addiction.

Dear Self,

### EXAMPLES

*Dear Self,*

*The change in our relationship was gradual. I didn't understand why, but if I look back I realize we were not sharing emotionally with each other, we weren't socializing with others, and John wasn't as sexually interested in me as he had been. But I didn't allow myself to think about it as I was busy with the kids and work. I knew he looked at porn, but I didn't think that was a bad thing. I took on a second job because of money problems, but didn't realize that he was lying to me about a very serious pornography addiction and acting out with women he'd met on the Internet. Since I became aware of this I realize that most of our relationship was based on lies. I am devastated and so angry at him for doing this to me and our family. I don't know if I can stay with him after all he's done. I trusted him 100 percent and now look where that has gotten me. I can't imagine ever trusting him again.*

. . . .

*Dear Self,*

*Our relationship started out with a lot of fun. I found him very exciting. I felt so special because he told me I was different, and I genuinely believed that I was different than his previous girlfriends. But I would catch him talking to other women or would question him as to why he came home so late from work. He'd give reasons that I now know were lies. He was often moody and blamed his moods on me being too demanding. So I would try harder to please him on every level, but nothing I did seemed to be good enough. I would get anxious about his absences and his criticisms of me and then the fun, attractive, and exciting sides of him would come back, and I'd feel better again and downplay my concerns since it felt so good again to see him happy with me. I realize now that I am probably no different than any other woman he's been with since he needs to feel special and the center of attention all the time.*

*I believe our relationship is a sham since I know he was cheating all along and has never been truthful with me. I feel manipulated and used.*

. . . .

*Dear Self,*

*I don't know how much our relationship has changed other than now I know that there has been chronic infidelity. I had my doubts but was afraid to say anything to her. I always felt inadequate, not good enough for her, and did not think the relationship would last. While I am now aware she has slept with nearly every man I considered a friend and probably some I don't even know about, I just feel more inadequate and not good enough for her. I want our relationship and she tells me she feels the same, but I am scared and afraid that she'll dupe me again. Boy was I fooled! How will I ever know it's okay to trust again?*

## MY LETTER ABOUT HOW I WANT TO BE TREATED IN MY RELATIONSHIP TODAY

Now write a letter to yourself about how you would like the relationship to look as you move forward. Even if you are uncertain whether you will stay with your partner or not, write about how you would like it to be in the meantime. Remember to keep the focus on *you* and write from an "I" perspective.

Dear Self,        I wish . . .      I like . . .      I want . . .      I need . . .

**EXAMPLE**

*Dear Self,*

*I would like to be treated with honesty and respect. What this means to me is to be told directly when there is a lie or half-truth and not be left guessing or second-guessing. I would like to know that my dreams for the future have value, and my feelings are important. I am scared about asking for what I need, but I want to try out new behavior and ask others to help me when I get afraid. I would like to be . . .*

## MY LETTER OF SELF-FORGIVENESS

In this final letter to yourself, you will focus your intentions on healing yourself from what you didn't or couldn't have known before. Many partners often find they are full of recriminations about the relationship and themselves. They believe they should have known they were being lied to or should have better trusted their instincts. Others falsely believe that if they had been prettier/more handsome, happier, or more sexual that they could have prevented the addiction from existing at all. These negative beliefs and assumptions, despite being inaccurate, leave partners feeling worse about themselves and make it harder to move ahead with their healing.

Write a letter to yourself forgiving yourself for being the person you were. If it is too difficult to forgive yourself at this time, write the letter as though you were able to forgive yourself at some time in the future. Write about what you'd forgive yourself for and remember to keep it in the present and personal.

**EXAMPLE**

*Dear Self,*

*It's been tough, it's been scary, and it hurts. I don't blame you for how you've tried to cope or the times in which you didn't cope. You are human. I forgive you for crying when what you were really feeling was anger. I forgive you for yelling when you were really just trying to get to the truth. I forgive you for not knowing what you didn't know. It's okay, we will get through this together.*

Taking the time to write these letters is a step in reaffirming who you are despite how terribly uncertain the future may feel. By staying vigilant during the process of self-discovery and reminding yourself you don't need to go through it alone, you begin to dispel the myths of addiction that have you believing you have to keep secrets and that no one will understand you. Many partners have walked the walk you are on and have come out ahead and stronger because of it. But it wouldn't have been possible if they hadn't taken the steps necessary to get honest with themselves. By completing this exercise, you have further committed yourself to the path of your journey of healing because your investment is in you and not the addiction.

# My Fluctuating Feelings

*The exercises in this section will help you to acknowledge the wide array of emotions common to living with sexual deception. They offer a structured format to begin to explore and face your emotional reality and recognize your acceptance or judgments about feelings. Many partners experience overwhelming emotions. Others describe being emotionally frozen and numb, which can hinder the ability to tolerate the discomfort brought on by unwelcome feelings.*

During times of acute crisis, experiencing a barrage of feelings is a normal reaction to the event. Sometimes the emotional response is so intolerable to the person experiencing it that he or she shuts down, or describes him- or herself as feeling numb. When feelings are ignored or not attended to, their impact can be that much more severe. Because the trauma is intimate in nature, the emotional work is more challenging as you are vacillating among multitudes of feelings related to the person with whom you may still be in a relationship. All of this adds to the uncertainty and anxiety you are feeling.

If for example, you believe your wife is a good mother, you may derive pleasant, warm feelings about that part of your relationship. However, when you think that she also cheated with other men, you understandably feel hurt, angry, and disgusted. Tolerating the two seemingly disparate feelings about the same person may confuse you. Or when you remember the images you came across on the computer and how you felt angry and compelled to search for more, all the while thinking your heart was going to break from the despair you felt. These fluctuating emotions often get too scary and the tendency is to avoid them altogether. On the other hand, you may be at the opposite extreme, feeling shut down, numb, frozen, and challenged by what you are feeling. Learning how to live with multiple and complex feelings simultaneously starts with identifying and labeling your emotions.

Feelings hurt most when they are denied, minimized, discounted, or experienced too intensely. If you have difficulty with feelings, most likely this reflects learned behavior from your childhood environment and societal messages. Experiencing emotion does not necessitate that action be taken. Feelings just *are*. What you do with a feeling is separate from the feeling itself. The emotion may influence the action you take, but it is not the action itself.

Learning to tolerate painful feelings is a skill. Management of feelings is a learned behavior and if learned poorly or inconsistently, then it makes the task more challenging today. If you tend to avoid or act out emotions rather than feel them, it is because it was safer to do so in the past. Today those coping skills betray you, since you have come to fear emotions and are less prepared to act in your own best interest. Recognize that undoing the learned patterns of the past while developing new skills will take time. Allow for a lot of trial and error during which you slowly become able to feel emotions that previously threatened you. Talking about how you feel, with supportive people, and learning to allow feelings to emerge can also help prevent or manage symptoms of depression and anxiety.

The following exercise is designed to help you identify those emotions more familiar to you during this time of crisis. Write down all those feelings that you have experienced since the crisis event. Use the following list as a guide. You may include other feelings/emotions not listed.

| | | | |
|---|---|---|---|
| Abandoned | Accepted | Affectionate | Alone |
| Angry | Annoyed | Anxious | Bitter |
| Brave | Calm | Caring | Confident |
| Conflicted | Courageous | Defeated | Desperate |
| Disappointed | Frightened | Ecstatic | Embarrassed |
| Enraged | Excited | Exposed | Foolish |
| Frantic | Furious | Fulfilled | Glad |
| Guilty | Happy | Helpless | Hopeful |
| Hopeless | Humiliated | Hurt | Impatient |
| Inadequate | Insecure | Intimidated | Irate |
| Irritated | Jealous | Joyful | Lonely |
| Patient | Regretful | Remorseful | Responsible |
| Sad | Serene | Shamed | Shocked |
| Stupid | Terrified | Thrilled | Tolerant |
| Worthy | Worried | | |

After reviewing all the feelings you have experienced since the crisis, select three of the most prevalent ones. With each feeling complete the following open-ended statement three separate times. *"I feel _____ about/that/when/of _____."* Give a different example each time, choosing the word that helps you best express the feeling.

**EXAMPLES**

I feel scared *about* . . . my future.

· · · ·

I feel scared *that* . . . my marriage will end.

· · · ·

I feel scared *when* . . . I think about others knowing.

· · · ·

I feel scared *of* . . . him.

- Which feelings do you experience as unwanted and try to avoid? Describe how you perceive yourself for having these feelings.

- Which feelings do you wish you could experience more readily? What makes it hard for you to experience these feelings?

View your feelings as a part of you—they are there as your friend, to guide you, not hurt you. They are neither right nor wrong; they describe your internal experience in the moment. Some feelings fluctuate; others stay on for a long time. Feelings are meant to serve as a barometer; however, they do not make up the whole of you, but rather a part of who you are. There are other ways you come to know yourself, and by working on your emotional intelligence you'll find you will be able to navigate any situation no matter how challenging it may be.

## Listening to My Body

*Having an awareness of where you carry your feelings in your body will help you become more aware of what your body is telling you. You will learn to identify how your body informs you of what it is experiencing so that you can see the relationship between unacknowledged feelings and the way they manifest in your physical self.*

Another way to deepen self-awareness is through the body. Sensations such as aches or pains, heart palpitations, a knot in the stomach, headaches, and muscle tension alert you that something is happening within the body. Naming the experience and recognizing other information it may offer you makes you more aware of the body's role in healing—especially if you have difficulty labeling a feeling and yet find yourself expressing emotion unexpectedly without any conscious idea why. Being aware of how your body responds to certain emotions may open up pathways of understanding previously unknown to you. Examples of this are tearing up when you hear someone else's story; laughing at sad events; or unexplained bouts of insomnia.

Human beings take in information through the use of our senses: sight, touch, hearing, smell, and taste. The body acts as a guide, a resource for information. By recognizing all your body has to offer, you can further access more data that will empower you to listen and honor what you need.

Having an awareness of where feelings are held in your body can help you become more mindful of what your body is telling you. The somatic (bodily) symptoms may help you respond to unexpressed emotional needs, allowing you to react more readily to situations that require attention.

In the previous exercise you identified the most predominant feelings you are experiencing since the crisis. Now list those. If identifying feelings is difficult, start by identifying five bodily sensations you commonly experience during times of stress.

In your journal, create a graphic similar to the one that follows. Now indicate on the drawing where you tend to experience sensations in the body. Label the feeling associated with the body part.

EXAMPLE

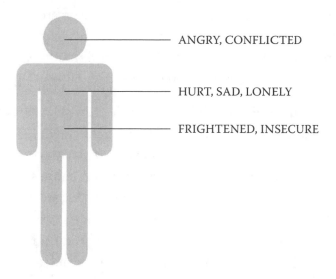

ANGRY, CONFLICTED

HURT, SAD, LONELY

FRIGHTENED, INSECURE

- What does completing this exercise tell you about your body and where you carry your emotions?

- Now that you've recognized certain areas of your physical being where you carry emotions, identify any body-related sensations. For example: if you find yourself experiencing frequent headaches, do you think it's about anger, loneliness, sadness? If you feel a stabbing pain in your side, do you think it is fear? What feelings might you connect to your back pain?

EXAMPLES

| Body Sensation(s) | Feeling(s) |
| --- | --- |
| 1. Shortness of breath | Anger, fury |
| 2. Back pain | Frightened, worried |
| 3. Tightness in shoulders | Hopelessness, insecurity |

Connecting your bodily sensations to your feelings is a vital skill in recognizing your emotions. Once you know your feelings, that awareness can lead you to recognizing your needs. The core issues of recovery are interconnected.

## THE IMPACT OF CHRONIC STRESS ON YOUR BODY

Not only will listening to your body tell you what you need, it can offer greater physical health. Unacknowledged feelings are enemies of the immune system. In a coupleship, acts of degradation, manipulation, secrecy, and shame take a toll over time. Sometimes it is the body that makes us aware of the assault this treatment is having in the form of health problems.

Chronic stress's impact on the nervous system can affect overall health and well-being; symptoms like chronic headaches and increased susceptibility to colds can indicate a high-stress environment reflective of a crisis or an unusual time in your life. With more exposure to chronic stress and especially without proper self-care and intervention, more serious health problems may develop. Stress has the ability to worsen many diseases that may be caused by other factors. Clearly, chronic stress has a strong impact on the immune system, particularly one that is already compromised. We believe many of the symptoms produced by stress are signs of partners feeling trapped by their circumstances without a sense of choice and options available to them.

Common illnesses and physical symptoms associated with stress include:

- Headaches or backaches
- Nausea, dizziness, fatigue
- Chest pain, rapid heartbeat
- Skin breakouts (hives, eczema)
- Asthma
- Chest pain
- Rapid heart rate
- Ulcers
- Hair loss
- Depression
- Diabetes
- Hyperthyroidism
- Rheumatoid arthritis
- Grinding teeth, temporomandibular joint disorder, commonly known as TMJ

- Diarrhea or constipation
- Insomnia
- Weight gain or loss
- Frequent colds or flu
- Shortness of breath
- High blood pressure
- Chronic back pain
- Sleep disturbance
- Sweats
- Anxiety disorder
- Heart disease
- Tooth and gum disease
- Fibromyalgia

EXAMPLE

*At the height of the insanity, I'd experience as many as seven facial tics in rapid succession. They would begin as small twitches near my eyes; they expanded to include more twitches in my cheeks and around my mouth. This continued for years. I must have looked like a contortionist. Once I began my recovery—and for me that included divorce—my symptoms disappeared and today only mildly reappear when I experience stressful situations.*

Certainly, you need to see a healthcare professional should you begin to experience any of these problems. At the same time, beginning with accepting your truth, identifying and sharing your feelings, and allowing yourself to get healthy support may be big factors in reducing many of these symptoms.

## Personal Strengths

*The foundation of how you see yourself is often greatly shaken by the experiences of sexual infidelity. "Personal Strengths" gives you the opportunity to recognize and honor your many talents and strengths that can help you address the crisis. The slightly unusual exercises in this section are nurturing and offer time for self-reflection. In addition to recognizing your positive attributes, you will have the chance to acknowledge the roles and interests you value, reminding you that there is more to life than what is occurring in your intimate relationship.*

It may be challenging at a time such as this to acknowledge your strengths, when your self-esteem is so compromised and you feel conflicted and vulnerable much of the time. It is time to shift gears and focus on those attributes that form the basis of who you are. Regardless of how beaten down you may feel, you have qualities and talents that are true about you and that are important to recognize and validate. As satisfying as it may feel when others acknowledge you, recovery is not waiting or depending on someone else's validation, but recognizing for yourself your inner strengths and positive attributes and working to make them more realized in your life today. These next exercises are designed to help you reconnect with the aspects of yourself that offer a stronger foundation to address your personal difficulties.

Find a comfortable place where you can be alone and there are few if any distractions. Perhaps it is a place in nature or a cozy chair or couch, possibly in front of a warm fire. Once you are in a comfortable place, write down and identify positive attributes that begin with each letter of the alphabet. (See examples below.) After identifying an attribute, pause and see if you can name any other attribute that begins with that specific letter. These may be characteristics that you have not tapped into for a long time, but that are still within you. It is possible that anything taken to an extreme is no longer healthy, but in moderation is positive. For example, thinking of yourself under "B" as *broadminded* may have been a part of your agreeing to engage in sexual behaviors that you didn't want to, or *caring* under "C" may mean having gone to the extreme—you care about others to the point of self-neglect. Allow yourself to recognize the parts of you that you value that have been positive at some point in your life. Enjoy knowing that what you write down is a part of you that you can appreciate and strengthen. It is easy in early recovery to see the dark side of things so, if you can, give yourself permission to take off those clouded glasses.

A   agile, affectionate, artistic

B   brave, broadminded

C   courageous, conscientious, caring

D   daring, dynamic

E   effervescent, eager, ethical

F   fun, forgiving, fatherly

G   good friend, grateful, gentle

H   humorous, health-conscious, honorable

I   industrious, intelligent, intuitive

J   joyful, joiner, just

K   knowledgeable, kind, kindred spirit

L   likeable, loving, laugh, leader

M   motherly, magnanimous, majestic, masterful

N   nice, natural, negotiator

O   open, observant, optimistic

P   polite, persevering, patient

Q   quiet, questioning, quick

R   risk-taker, reasonable, respectful

S   sincere, studious, sensual

T   tender, thoughtful, teachable

U   understanding, unstoppable, upbeat

V   vigilant, verbal, versatile

W   wise, willing, witty

X   xtraordinary, xemplary ☺

Y   youthful

Z   zestful, zany

• Select five attributes that you listed that you would most like to have acknowledged or strengthened at this time in your recovery. Write an affirmation from those.

• Let's say you choose specific words from A, C, I, N, and W. Take those words and create an affirmation by beginning the sentence with "*I am . . .*" Ultimately, you want to do this with all the letters. When doing this exercise keep the affirmations in the present, personal, and positive (the three "P"s.) Remember you can add words like *becoming* or *allowing myself to* since at times it may be hard to own these things as true for you today.

**EXAMPLES**

| | |
|---|---|
| Artistic | *I am artistic.* Or, *I am becoming more artistic.* |
| Courageous | *I am courageous.* Or, *I am becoming more courageous.* |
| Intuitive | *I am intuitive.* |
| Negotiator | *I am a negotiator.* |
| Wise | *I am wise.* |

- Write these affirmations down on separate index cards or in your handheld device. If you use cards, place them in strategic places. This could be in your purse or wallet, on the bathroom mirror, on the front of your computer, on the dashboard of your car, or on your phone. Wherever you choose to place your affirmations, at least three times during the day stop to read each statement, pausing as you go from one to the next. After each individual statement add "Yes, I am." So you find yourself saying something such as, "I am artistic. [Pause] Yes, I am." This will reinforce the statement. Then go on to the next statement. Do not rush. As awkward or silly as it may seem, affirmations, when repeated regularly, become internalized and a part of your belief system. They will replace the faulty, negative thinking that erodes your self-worth. After you work with the initial five affirmations for at least two weeks, change them or add new ones to your list.

## ROLES AND INTERESTS

In addition to recognizing your positive attributes, it is important to acknowledge the roles and interests you value in your life. Examples of roles are parent, daughter, wife/husband/ partner, brother, sister, business owner, entrepreneur, dancer, photographer, employee, community/church volunteer, etc.

Name the variety of roles in your life and describe what you like about yourself when in these roles.

Since you most likely fill many roles and have a variety of interests, some of these offer more joy, value, or meaning than others. Remember, this is not the time to focus on what is missing or what creates pain and hurt, but to recognize that which presently supports your sense of self.

Complete each of the following statements three times. Repeating these statements helps to reinforce and validate your experience.

- *I enjoy* (e.g., fishing, reading, art).
- *I am competent at* (e.g., bridge, carpentry, cooking).

- *I take pride in* (e.g., being a parent, my work, my education).
- *My _____ is important to me* (e.g., my pet, my political activism, etc.).

- What do you like about yourself when you actively participate in these interests?

Taking an inventory of your strengths and assessing your interests and various roles allow you to broaden your perspective about who you really are, not just how you feel as a result of this unfortunate crisis. Having the fortitude to see all of who you are makes you more adept at facing what is ahead of you. By taking into account your strengths, you create options for how to handle situations.

# CHAPTER THREE

# My Part of the Dance

You have begun the process of taking control of your recovery. We hope by now you are building a support system for yourself and have begun to claim your reality and see a future for yourself regardless of where the relationship may be at this moment. While you still have serious concerns and there is still much to be answered, it is now time to look at your behaviors and what you do that contributes to your part of the addictive cycle. The following exercises will assist you in recognizing faulty thinking and unhealthy behaviors that sabotage your ability to feel good about yourself. They will also support you in developing new ways of relating and being that empower you to move forward in your life.

# A: Emotional Challenges

## Stepping Out of Reaction into Action

*"Stepping Out of Reaction into Action" validates how easy it is to engage in noneffective responses to stressful situations and at the same time helps you understand how you may have a history that triggers you to act in self-defeating behaviors. But more importantly, it offers you a structure so that you can respond from a place of strength versus reactivity when you experience a trigger.*

One of the more challenging aspects you've faced and may encounter again is the destabilizing effect of stumbling upon the suspicious, duplicitous behavior(s) of the addict. Often in recovery, especially within the first few years, triggers (yours) and slips (addict's) occur. Planning for one means anticipating how you might react and preparing for how you'd like to handle it. Understanding how you tend to address upsetting situations is useful in uncovering common responses, which are often ineffective when coping with sex addiction. Learning about yourself and how you can change your patterns lessens the impact of addiction and frees you to become the person you want to be.

When a disturbing event happens, such as finding an unexplained phone number or a hotel receipt, an automatic, initial response is disbelief and shock that this is occurring. An urge to confront the addict often follows as an attempt to quell the disturbance facing you. Secrets and lies are the drivers of the sexual behavior, which in turn is an immediate trigger for you. Your security in the relationship has already been disrupted by discovery and/or disclosure, and you are on alert for any possible further exposure by the addict.

Sometimes your impulse toward action gets directed inward at yourself. You fear addressing your concerns with your partner because he or she won't be honest and may ignore your questions or blame you for looking for information and not trusting him or her. You may make excuses or avoid it all together because you want the problem to go away. You tell yourself if you don't make a big deal of it, it will disappear on its own. This failure to act is still an action; it's the action of inaction. Unease sets in and an urge to distract with other responsibilities takes over. Work, kids, household projects, or addictive behaviors such as eating, shopping, and drinking help you to avoid facing the disturbing information you have found. Maintaining the outward appearance keeps you believing all is okay. It also fosters a sense of control, offsetting the reality that is your partner's sex addiction, over which little to no control exists.

Whether you react with action directed at the addict through confrontation, or inaction, ignoring the distress and criticizing yourself for having suspicions, you are at risk for additional emotional vulnerability and loss of control. Your attempts to resolve the problem prove ineffective, resulting in pain, confusion, despair, and helplessness. When the action is directed at the addict, "He needs to explain his behavior to me so I can feel better, and admit he's wrong and get help," the outcome depends upon your partner. If, through denial and avoidance, "I can't do anything about it, so why bother," you demonstrate a helpless attitude and are at the mercy of further victimization by triggering events, then you will continue to short-circuit your emotional response unless you learn other adaptive ways to address triggering events.

Tolerating and processing unwelcome emotional states is a lifelong skill that ideally develops in childhood. When children are taught healthy ranges of emotional expression, it is because their caregivers are able to model acceptance and provide self-soothing strategies to them. This allows for safety in expressing distressing feelings. Caregivers who provide nurturing environments also teach the child when it is time to shift away from the distress. Like shifting gears in a car, the caregiver serves as the model for the child for when it is okay to move from one emotion to the next. However, when children are exposed to environments that are not affirming or do not validate them, then experiences of distress and discomfort are met with fear and anger. In turn, children learn that their needs for comfort, attention, direction, and healthy self-soothing are wrong or bad, resulting in a negative self-image. Children in these types of households learn that emotional distress is something to fear, avoid, flee from, or fight, with the result that unacceptable feelings are truncated, aborted, or stunted. Maladaptive ways to handle distress, also known as defensive strategies, are formed and have an effect on the developing child's sense of security. Continuing into adulthood, these defensive strategies become the reflexive, automatic responses to all life-threatening triggers. Defensive coping skills that were safe ways of adapting in childhood, serving to block and/ or hide other reactions or feelings children experienced form the way adults think, feel, and approach life-threatening issues in the present.

Eventually, the truth always has a way of revealing itself. Until you face your tendency to avoid or run from truth, which is an old skill you've used repeatedly, it will be difficult to effect meaningful change in yourself or your relationship to the addict. You will explore this dynamic in greater detail as you examine how impulsive or frozen responses affect you. By identifying your initial feelings, impulses, and urges, and seeing how automatic yet maladaptive behaviors influence your handling of problems, you will see that newer ways to work with distress are needed. You will also explore the additional feelings, thoughts, and ideas that may be underlying your defenses. These new ways of thinking and responding offer opportunities to develop healthier habits of relating that will empower you and bring greater health to your relationship.

## TRIGGERING EVENT

### EXAMPLES

*You come across an unexplained email account, phone number, or bill.*

· · · ·

*An accidental call comes to your cell phone from your spouse and you overhear him having sex with another woman.*

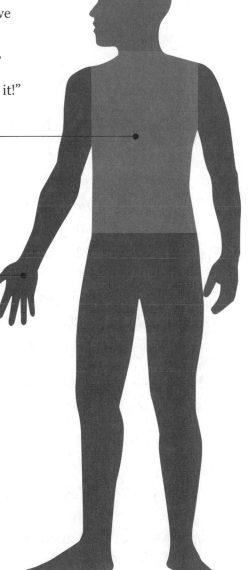

**Initial response:** (Often happens in your thinking) negative self-talk and judgments.

- "How dare she!"
- "What is this?"
- "What am I going to do?"
- "I can't believe it!"

**Feelings/Body Sensations**

- Shock
- Rage
- Helplessness
- Despair
- Anger
- Body: stomach upset, headache, fatigue, cramps

**Reaction**

*Actions*

- Search all bills.
- Call him at work.
- Confront her.
- Call attorney and file divorce papers.
- Drive to where he is at that moment.

*Inactions*

- Sleep
- Avoid it and don't bring it up with him.
- Pretend it doesn't matter.
- Clean.
- Focus on children.
- Repress thoughts and feelings about what you found.

**Outcome:** The action/inaction from the triggering event. The behaviors and attitudes you adopt in response to the situation.

- Stalemate
- Inconclusive data
- Self-doubt
- No resolution
- Stuck

- Ongoing distress
- Lying
- Regret about behaviors you took
- No plan
- Back where you started from but feel worse

Identify a triggering event or situation that was most disturbing between you and the addict.

EXAMPLE

*I found a lipstick in the car that didn't belong to me.*

- Recall what happened next and the dialogue you had with yourself.

EXAMPLE

*Oh my God! I can't believe this! Where did this come from? I don't recognize this! Maybe it's mine. It can't be. I don't wear this color. Whose is it? What is George going to say this time? He'll try to tell me it's mine. You no good ^&$%.*

These responses may be what you thought, but what if this is only part of what you experienced?

- How did you feel?

EXAMPLE

*Shock, disbelief, outrage, fear.*

- What did you notice in your body? The body also informs you of feelings (emotions) and sensations (physical feelings).

EXAMPLE

*Immediately my head started pounding. So many thoughts at once!*

· · · ·

*I ran to the bathroom because I felt sick to my stomach. I had diarrhea. I had butterflies in my stomach. My heart was racing and my blood pressure went up. I had to call the doctor and increase my medication. I felt fatigued and I found myself falling asleep.*

• How did you act?

EXAMPLE
*I started rummaging through his cell phone records, calling his friend, and asking him what he thought.*

• What was your initial reaction? Was it a thought, feeling, or sensation?

• What type of behavior did you take? Action or inaction?

• What was the outcome when you acted on the impulse? Did it help solve the problem?

• How did you feel afterward?

• Drawing your own graphic, walk through the steps above again and now take notice of your thoughts, feelings, and reactions. Were you acting from your thoughts (head)?

• What was the initial feeling? Were there other feelings beyond the initial one?

• Were you tempted to take action or not?

• What could help you to sit with the experience before acting or avoiding?

Understanding your automatic responses and learning new ways to manage them will better help you to decide how to respond to a trigger or a slip. In this way, you become better able to handle situations that used to overwhelm you and your overall well-being will improve.

# Unraveling the Myths of Control

*In this section, we introduce the many ways you have likely attempted to control or change*

*your partner's behavior. In the immediate moment you may have experienced a sense of empowerment, but in the long run, your attempts were ineffective and your sense of power an illusion. Recognizing your controlling behavior is a major step in letting go of self-defeating behaviors and freeing you up for greater self-care.*

As an attempt to bring stability and self-protection to the insidious violation of trust, the betrayed partner often and unknowingly responds to day-to-day concerns by engaging in behaviors focused on altering or changing the addict. When done repeatedly over time, these behaviors begin to feel normal, yet in reality are ways to protect you from the impact of a silent addiction not yet fully realized. These protective mechanisms served you well when you didn't know you were being robbed of your sense of control and safety, but in recovery, these attempts at control will keep you from true self-protection and healing.

Controlling behavior is the manipulation of people, places, and things. It is also a defense against shame, as you feel responsible to "fix" the addict and protect him or her from self-destructive habits. The benefit to you is that it imparts a sense of power at a time in your life when you are overwhelmed with fear and helplessness. At a time of desperation it seems like a quick fix. In the moment you don't feel a sense of inadequacy; if anything, you feel empowered. But this is an illusion since you fundamentally can't change another's thinking or actions and soon enough the behaviors return.

Attempts at control can be expressed in either overt or subtle ways. Most likely you and your partner developed a pattern of communication that is indirect and ultimately futile. For your part, nothing changed in the relationship because the solution rested with the addict and not yourself. One partner in recovery described it this way:

> *"Before I began recovery I would say the same things over and over to my partner such as 'I need you to communicate with me more.' I expected him to change. Now in recovery the words might be the same, but I expect* me *to change. If he doesn't listen, I take care of me, whereas in the past I would chase him till I got what I wanted until the same thing would happen again. Now, we both have better tools to deal with our problems of communicating, but for me I understand that I am responsible for taking care of my needs first, not him."*

What follows are some common coping behaviors partners reported while living with a sex addict.

- Throwing out the stash: *I would find his porn and throw it away.*

- Arguing/Confronting the behaviors: *I told her that flirting was not okay and she'd do it again and again.*

- Avoiding communication: *I knew he was around less, but I accepted it and didn't ask questions.*

- Canceling plans: *There were times I'd cancel plans and I would stay home thinking that would make it harder for him to make excuses to go out. Or I thought if I was home he wouldn't get on the Internet.*

- Silent treatment: *I knew this hurt him and I wanted to punish him for lying.*

- Relocating: *We moved from one city after another, telling our family it was always for my job or hers, as if it were a promotion for us. We would start over, but nothing ever changed.*

- Lying: *I would lie to her and tell her she had to stay home to be with the kids and then I would stay at work late on the night when I was pretty sure she had plans to meet her lover.*

- Making threats: *I threatened to tell the kids, tell his parents, tell his boss, to divorce, to go to his lover's house, and even to have my own affairs.*

- Sexual manipulation: *Flirting with others or threatening to be sexual with others to create jealousy thinking that would get him more focused on me; acting or dressing sexy to gain or maintain his attention; pretending I was into certain types of sexual acts that I hated just to try and keep him at home; and agreeing to have sex when I didn't want to.*

- Having secrets: *Withholding information reinforces the belief that I have some power over my partner.*

- Guilting/Shaming: *I would say hurtful things to trigger his guilt and shame, thinking that would make him stop his behaviors.*

- Maintaining aggressive anger response: *I would think that my obvious anger was so intimidating that she wouldn't dare to do something to upset me.*

- Take a look at the list above and write in your journal all of the ways in which you have attempted to control or manipulate the behavior of your partner. This exercise highlights how the relationship negatively affected you as you tried to make sense of the addictive behaviors.

• Now list examples of your attempts to change the behavior of the addict.

EXAMPLE

**Behavior change sought:** *Stop my husband from staying out late after work.*

**What you did:** *Tried to get him to commit to a time he would be home and reminded him of other times he was late.*

**Outcome:** *It happened again and I gave him the cold shoulder. I didn't talk to him for three days.*

Controlling is ultimately ineffective and harmful, and leads to feelings of futility and failure. As you explore how you got here, try not to judge yourself. Be empathetic. Your actions are understandable. Controlling behaviors are an attempt to bring safety to situations that feel threatening. The illusion of control has you believing you can change the addict. It is in letting go of controlling behavior that you can refocus on you and what you need and allow your partner to take responsibility for his or her actions. Change like this is hard and often slow. Moving ahead means trying to learn new behaviors and challenging those that no longer work for you by learning to focus on you and what you can change—that is where true healing and growth occur.

## My Relationship with Anger

*Now you will learn to recognize both the positive aspects of your anger and how it can also be destructive. Most partners' relationships with anger are often distorted, misplaced, or denied. You certainly have the right to be angry, but this exercise assists you to determine whether your expression of anger is helpful or hurtful and offers you direction to be able to use anger in a constructive manner.*

Anger is a feeling that can be difficult to tolerate, making it an emotion that you either overly identify with or choose to avoid. You may vacillate between the two extremes. The intensity and distortion of anger is very significant, so it's important to explore in greater detail the meaning, positive uses of, and some of the common destructive forms it can take.

Looking at the continuum below, how would you describe your experience of anger?

1 ——————————————————— 5 ———————————————————10
Avoidant　　　　Rarely Angry　　　Appropriately Angry　　　Often Angry　　　Rage

Anger may now be the predominant emotion you experience since the crisis of discovery. Confronting sexual deception is a traumatic process that affects your relationship and your self-esteem and you have the right to be angry; your reasons are justified. You're angry for being betrayed, and for the disregard your partner had for you and the relationship. You're angry about how your family and your health have been affected or you're angry at yourself for the loyalty you had for someone who has duped you with lies. You are angry for having wasted the best years of your life, or worse, for knowing about his or her behaviors and staying in the relationship anyway. For many partners, this anger is a difficult and threatening emotion to manage and/or tolerate.

Destructive forms of anger are harmful, threatening, hidden, and abusive, preventing you from overcoming your losses. Our goal is to help you 1) understand healthy use of anger and validate its importance in your life; 2) explore your relationship to anger; and 3) underscore the common pitfalls many partners encounter.

## HEALTHY ANGER

Anger is an emotion and a biologically occurring event. It exists in all of us, and it's our relationship to it that determines how we will use it. It informs us as to our likes and dislikes. Its positive attributes serve as protection from threat and it can mobilize us into action. However, it doesn't always involve an action; it could inform us not to act since to do so may cause injury. Acknowledgment and validation occur before action. Simply knowing what it is you're feeling is enough.

- Describe how you express anger. Do you find you express it differently in different areas of your life? (Parenting, work, friends, family.)

- What areas do you find you feel more confident or certain about your expression of anger?

- How have you experienced anger now that you know your partner has cheated on you? Do you find this is or isn't working for you?

## ANGER DISTORTION

Distorted anger exists along a continuum from avoidance to frustration to rage. At this point in your life, you may identify with one end of the spectrum versus the other, or you may jump between the two, never knowing for sure what to expect of yourself. Anger becomes an emotion that you dread because it is unpredictable and unsafe.

Perhaps you are someone whose anger builds up and you find yourself exploding irrationally, making you feel out of control. Or perhaps you are completely anger-avoidant. You fear losing control or being punished for expressing anger. Worse, you believe you will be left, ignored, or laughed at for showing how upset you are with someone. Perhaps you frequently move all over the continuum. Unfortunately by now your anger is often both distorted and fueled by myriad other feelings and negative thoughts. Even if your partner's behavior has stopped, you don't just let go of your anger. The losses and the betrayal have been significant. A part of your healing is being able to tolerate your anger without engaging in self-defeating or self-destructive behavior.

## RAGE

On the far end of the anger spectrum is rage, a commonly impulsive, destructive, and often physical form of anger. Acts of rage are meant to cause immediate pain to another person.

Characteristics of rage include,

- Hitting
- Punching
- Damaging property
- Throwing things
- Stalking

Perhaps you've confronted a new lie or found another voice mail from an escort service and you find yourself doing things you never would have imagined yourself doing, such as,

- Using GPS to track your partner's whereabouts;
- Surreptitiously putting monitoring devices on phone, email, computer;

- Calling former affair partner/escorts and telling them off;

- Slashing tires;

- Keying his or her car; or

- Going to establishments your partner frequents hoping to catch and/or confront him or her there.

During the time you are in a rage you feel powerful because adrenaline floods your system and creates a high that temporarily makes you believe your behavior is justified and no one is being harmed. You believe you are defending yourself from injury and you just want your partner to feel the pain he or she has inflicted upon you.

Rage is often a cover-up for many other feelings. Shame, embarrassment, humiliation, fear, and sadness are right there along with your rage. It is understandable that you are feeling all of those emotions. Betrayal hurts. It hurts more deeply than anything you have ever known. But the aftermath of your rageful actions only compounds all the buried and conflicting emotions and further deepens your despair and suffering. In the long run, the act of rage will only hurt you. It's healthier to find something constructive to do with that rage. You deserve better than to act on it and then have to endure the consequences.

## SIDEWAYS ANGER (PASSIVE AGGRESSIVE)

Within the anger continuum is sideways anger, also referred to as passive aggression. It may take the form of vengeful fantasies and indirect expressions of your distress. Characteristics of this type of anger include,

- Subtle versus blatant actions, attitudes, or thoughts;

- Verbal versus nonverbal expressions, facial expressions;

- Threats, screaming, and blaming;

- Giving the cold shoulder;

- Deflecting anger toward others, often the innocent;

- Sarcasm;

- Suspicions, waiting for him or her to act out again;

- Socially avoidant of others;

- Talking negatively about your partner;

- Ruminating and having contemptuous thoughts; and/or
- Looking for opportunities where he or she may fail.

Sideways anger can be extremely destructive because it can simmer beneath the surface and be methodical and vengeful. Chronically repeating this type of behavior leads to feelings of contempt and disconnection in the relationship and creates little opportunity for change and growth.

### EXAMPLES

*When I thought he was with a woman, I would get her phone number and call incessantly and then hang up.*

. . . .

*I had an affair myself to show her.*

. . . .

*I verbally raged at my kids for things that had nothing to do with them.*

. . . .

*I spent thousands of dollars shopping when I believed he was lying to me.*

. . . .

*I screamed he was a pervert so others could hear me.*

. . . .

*I told her she was a whore.*

. . . .

*I looked for him to mess up and fail in his program so I could tell him "see I told you so!"*

Sideways anger, fueled by a deep-seated desire for revenge, can provide fleeting moments of vindication and satisfaction. However, in the end, indirectly expressing your anger only lessens your self-respect, dignity, and self-esteem and the potential fallout and/or consequences can be devastating.

## ANGER AVOIDANCE

Some partners say they just don't feel angry; some say they feel defeated, numb, or do what they can to stay distracted from letting their anger surface. Others don't acknowledge ever feeling the emotion. They may acknowledge that they *should* feel angry, but aren't. Most likely, avoidance is a learned response to stress, a response that is often adopted in childhood and/or is the consequence of long-term, hurtful adult relationships. Anger avoidance is often a part of low-grade chronic depression (dysthymia) or anxiety. You may have learned that responding to a bad situation with judicious anger didn't change the predicament; you only felt helpless. When anger doesn't restore your sense of control over the environment you eventually begin to feel apathetic; you come to believe that nothing good will ever come of it, so why expend the energy to just feel more battered.

You may be using the distraction of staying busy to help stuff your anger. Busyness is often demonstrated through housework, shuffling kids to activities and appointments, shopping, or work. Some people act out their busyness by getting overly involved in their jobs and community. It could mean that you spend hours at the health club or on the computer. By themselves, none of these behaviors is bad, and in fact they are often esteemed. But involvement that is excessive and done in a way to avoid the challenges in your relationship and family merely serves as an unhealthy diversion.

Characteristics of anger avoidance include,

- Turning inward, blaming self;
- Being unconscious that you have anger at all;
- Having negative beliefs about expressing anger;
- Taking a victim-like stance (leaving you prone to being hurt again);
- Using distraction behaviors;
- Procrastinating.

To talk yourself out of anger you engage in both distorted thinking and inaction.

**EXAMPLES**

*Maybe I'm expecting too much.*

. . . .

*What's wrong with what I said?*

. . . .

*Give her the benefit of the doubt.*

. . . .

*Mask anger with tears.*

. . . .

*Can't hold the addict accountable for his or her actions.*

. . . .

*Avoid bringing up suspicions.*

For those who express anger in a sideways manner or are anger-avoidant it is healthy to be able to own your anger with clarity and directness. Write down the expressions of anger you identify with.

Rageful                    Sideways Anger                    Anger-Avoidant


- Give examples of how you have acted out in rage. How has your rageful behavior hurt you?

EXAMPLE

*I did these outrageous things and in the long run it just made me look like the crazy one. Then I became depressed and began to question myself and not him.*


- Give examples of how you have acted out in sideways anger. How has sideways anger hurt you?

EXAMPLE

*I'm in a constant state of mental obsession. I do things I'd never want others to know about so I have this vengeful secret life.*


- Give examples of how you have been anger-avoidant. What do you tell yourself to avoid getting angry?

EXAMPLE

*I will lose control like my mother and be told I'm crazy. What does it matter if I get angry? He'll act out anyway.*


- How has avoiding anger hurt you?

EXAMPLE

*It made me unprepared for how to defend myself when I was lied to. I didn't know what to think or say. I just forgave and moved on.*


- Do you flip back and forth from avoiding anger to being enraged? If so, give examples of how you have flipped back and forth.

• How has your all-or-nothing approach to anger hurt you?

**EXAMPLE**

*When I would learn he'd acted out again I would vacillate between telling myself not to say anything to sneaking into his workplace and checking his accounts and then setting up an argument intending to catch him in a lie. Then I'd flip out and call him all sorts of names. I couldn't predict how I was going to act, nor did I ever have a plan to stop this pattern of reaction to his hurtful behaviors. I couldn't get him to stop, nor could I stop myself!*

• What are situations where it would have been appropriate for you to express your anger and you did not?

**EXAMPLES**

*When he yelled at me for questioning the phone bill, I clammed up.*

. . . .

*When she came home late I acted as if I was asleep and didn't tell her I was mad.*

• Do you believe you have a problem with anger? The goal is not to get rid of anger as a feeling, but to capitalize on its energy.

Below are a few examples of positive steps to take that lead to the healthy expression of anger.

Write down all of the actions that you are willing to do.

• Become curious about your anger patterns.

• Learn about constructive expressions of anger.

• Challenge your destructive views on anger.

• Talk about your feelings in ways that focus on you and your feelings.

• Do soothing activities.

• Use slogans from a/your/his/her twelve-step program.

• Create bottom lines for your anger; have an agreement with yourself that you uphold no matter what.

The following are examples of constructive expressions of anger. List all those that you are willing to try.

- Pound pillows.
- Go for a walk, run, or other physical activity.
- Call a friend and talk about it.
- Journal or draw your emotions.
- Write a venomous letter, then burn it or tear it up.
- Sit with the anger for twenty to thirty minutes to allow emotions to subside.
- Punch a punching bag.
- Blow up balloons and then pop them.
- Take a kickboxing, karate, or self-defense class.
- Breathe, breathe, breathe.

Constructive use of anger means accessing choices and being able to think through the consequences before acting. When you make healthy choices, you empower yourself. A healthy expression of anger is often consistent with your values about how you want to be treated and how you treat others and leads to healing, growth, and change, which results in greater self-respect.

## The Myth of Perfectionism

*It is extremely common to push yourself toward being 150 percent, to be the perfect partner in an attempt to get your partner's or society's love and approval. Yet perfectionism tends to only reinforce the belief that who you are is not good enough. It is time to let go of such thinking. This exercise will assist you in coming to a greater acceptance of who you are and being your true self.*

Perfectionism is a common response to emotional pain. At some point in your life you learned to push yourself to excel, to be the best—be it the best mother, father, daughter, son, wife, husband, worker, friend, or student. In its healthy form, perfectionism drives people toward goals. Perfectionists are individuals who are motivated toward accomplishments. Although perfectionists and high-achievers share common traits, high-achievers have greater self-esteem and set more realistic goals. They also demonstrate greater flexibility when roadblocks arise.

In its unhealthy form, perfectionism is manifested in negative thinking and self-defeating behaviors. Irrational beliefs fuel perfectionist traits and center on acquiring approval. "If I am perfect, I will be loved and cared for." If you don't identify as someone who is seeking approval, your perfectionism may be about avoiding rejection. "I try to be the perfect wife so he won't leave me." The reinforcing aspect to the rigid belief system that drives perfectionism is that "no matter what I do, it is never good enough" so "I have to keep pushing harder and harder."

Perfectionism also means there is no room for mistakes or vulnerability. This is also referred to as "all-or-nothing" or "black-and-white" thinking. Anything less than 150 percent becomes unacceptable. It would mean failure, and for you that failure means possible rejection and abandonment. When there is a problem in the relationship, rather than risking greater upheaval, you believe that it is you who has to give more or find the answers rather than expecting your partner to do so.

Sadly, most perfectionists have no internal sense of limits. With shame and fear constantly nipping at their heels, they are always measuring their perceived performance against how others see them. Their sense of self is related to a standard or judgment borne of others' expectations of them. The hypervigilance and preoccupation about not being good enough reflects the residue left from people who sought power over them by threatening to reject and abandon them, and whose love and approval was conditional. There is never a time or place to rest or to have inner joy and satisfaction.

You are a perfectionist if in your mind you never measure up. As a result, you compare yourself with others and your views are of extremes: good versus bad, better versus worse, or more versus less. Inevitably, you end up feeling the lesser for the comparison because the ideal of who you should be is forever outside your reach. Comparing yourself with others is one of the primary ways you continue to foster more shame and low self-esteem.

A perfectionist trait in a partnership where addiction exists requires a great deal of time and energy and results in loneliness and isolation. When you engage in a task to the degree it takes to do it "perfectly," it interferes with other relationships and takes a toll on you physically and emotionally. More time is invested in preserving the ideal, and you feel yourself being pushed to succeed despite being unhappy in the process.

Describe ways in which you engage in perfectionist behavior or attitudes.

**EXAMPLES**

*I compulsively exercise and have used cosmetic surgery to be the perfect sexual partner.*

· · · ·

*I am the perfect mother, taking my kids to every possible event or activity, having healthy food in the house, and keeping an impeccable house.*

It is likely you have been doing this for so long you don't recognize there are false beliefs that support your behavior. It is important to pause and seriously reflect on what is underlying this behavior.

Think of your perfectionism as fear-based, and ask yourself, what is the false belief you tell yourself? Then identify your fear. Give two examples.

**EXAMPLES**

Thought: *I tell myself if I am good enough, he won't stray.*

Feeling: *I fear he will act out.*

· · · ·

Thought: *I tell myself he won't have anything to complain about, and will be happier, and if he's happier he won't spend so much time on the Internet.*

Feeling: *I fear that I am responsible for his acting out.*

If you have trouble identifying the thoughts or feelings, begin with recognizing your perfectionist behavior and then keep asking yourself, "What is the false belief underlying my behavior?" and "What are the feelings or fears associated with that behavior?"

You'll find that by setting and maintaining healthy internal boundaries and tapping into your own self-worth you will be better able to counteract faulty thinking. As your integrity strengthens, it will give you more confidence in speaking what is true for you.

All your perfectionism and over-functioning are not going to change the fact that your partner has this problem, nor will it get your partner into his or her own recovery or keep him or her there. It is imperative that you accept that your partner's behavior is not about you or your worth, your actions, or inactions.

Recognize that you may do many things well, but you are paying a high price if you hold onto truths that are built on false premises.

Write down those items from the following list that identify the negative consequence for your perfectionism.

- Interferes with time with friends.
- Interferes with knowing myself.
- Interferes with time with partner.
- Interferes with time with children.
- Makes me tired and stressed.
- Makes me chronically criticize myself.
- Makes me feel inadequate.
- Makes me feel helpless and think, "Why bother trying to change."
- Other.

The following are examples of both affirmations and beliefs that counteract perfectionist thinking.

*I am doing my best and that is good enough.*

*I am good enough.*

*Mistakes are a part of my humanness.*

*I deserve more time with my children/friends/partner.*

*There is always more to do; it can wait.*

*Nothing bad happens because I am less than perfect.*

*We are all humanly imperfect.*

*I will have more time to enjoy people and things when I let go of my perfectionism.*

*My perfectionism only fuels a false illusion.*

*I choose reality.*

*This shall pass.*

*More than one thing is true at the same time.*

*It's okay to have more than one feeling about this situation.*

*I don't have to have the answers right now.*

*I can be patient with myself.*

Write down those affirmations from the list above that you are willing to incorporate into your self-talk. And then identify any additional messages that would be helpful to you.

In addition to challenging perfectionist thinking, there are behaviors that you will want to diminish and/or enhance to create healthier behavior. The following are examples that others in recovery have noted.

## Diminishing Behaviors

*Shorten my " to do" list.*

*Not clean house prior to housekeeper coming.*

*Not smile when angry, sad, or scared.*

*Stop seeking the perfect romantic outfit.*

*Reconsider cosmetic surgery that I am thinking about.*

*Don't use the words "I'm fine."*

## Enhancing Behaviors

*Say what I really feel.*

*Own my behavior.*

*Ask myself what I need or want.*

*Take time out in the day for me.*

*Incorporate meditation into my self-care.*

The gift that comes with letting go of your perfectionism is that you no longer carry the burden, keep up pretenses, and/or run from yourself. It gives you the opportunity to appreciate and embrace your humanness.

## B: Perception Challenges

## Coping or Defending: The Paradox of Facing Your Reality

*This section gives you the opportunity to look at whether or not your coping strategies are helpful to you. Everyone has defensive strategies they employ, but while useful in the beginning they often become ineffectual and even self-defeating. Completing this exercise will help you recognize when you are engaged in any self-defeating behavior and begin to steer you toward healthy self-care.*

Given the confusion, fear, anger, and pain that are associated with the crisis in your life, it is only normal you'd want to defend or distract yourself from reality. Defenses are strategies used by individuals to cope with reality and maintain an intact self-image. They are a necessary attribute of one's humanness. Defenses have the potential to cover and protect your feelings, to resist a painful reality, and/or to help you feel a greater sense of security.

While some defenses are more conscious, others, such as dissociation are not—both have short-term advantages. They often cause long-term problems in relationships and other areas of living when they become the predominant style of coping. Defenses understandably begin as a form of self-protection, becoming a coping skill, but it often takes on a life of its own and when that happens, it has outlived its usefulness and has very likely become self-sabotaging and hurtful.

It is likely the coping behaviors you are using are ones you learned at other vulnerable moments in your life. If you grew up in a household full of conflict, you may have found the best way to stay safe was to become very quiet and say nothing. Or you may have used humor to defuse a situation. Or if you previously experienced a lot of sadness, you may have found comfort in overeating or in finding numerous ways to stay busy to distance yourself from the pain. It's possible these behaviors have been with you a long time, and while they initially served a purpose, the key is to identify and recognize how they are getting in the way of how you want to live your life today.

The following are a variety of common defenses:

- Anger
- Silence
- Intellectualizing
- Smoking
- Busyness
- Magical thinking
- Gambling

- Rage
- Humor
- Isolation
- Food
- Smiling
- Exercise
- Shopping

- Ambivalence
- Sarcasm
- Minimizing
- Work
- Perfectionism
- Alcohol/other drugs

While you may have used several of the defenses listed above at some time in your life, note the ones that you have been using most recently, particularly since you became aware of this problem. Then list the defenses you noted and identify what you gain by utilizing this defense and what the cost is to you.

**EXAMPLES**

*The gain to my perpetual smile is that others believe everything is okay; but I lose honesty with others and myself.*

· · · ·

*I gain distance from the problem with my busyness, but it only postpones the reality, the inevitable, making my situation even more complicated.*

- As you go through your day, pay attention to when you engage in these specific defenses and identify the feelings or fears you are trying to avoid.

Depending on the situation, find a way to acknowledge rather than to use the defense. Reach out to one of your safe people to let him or her know your thoughts and feelings. You may want to create a specific area in your journal where you note how you are using your defenses to block your pain. Or engage in a mindfulness exercise of deep breathing or meditation. Certainly, if you're feeling strong and safe, speaking your truth and reality to the one you are reacting to may be the most constructive response.

# Removing the Veil of Denial

*Here we will assist you in being empathetic to your denial as a form of self-protection. You will get to recognize both the pros and the cons. This is a process of helping you look beyond the fears and become more honest with yourself.*

A significant part of acting out with an addictive behavior is being in denial about the seriousness of the behavior and the consequences. Not only does the person acting out engage in the defense of denial, so do partners.

Words spoken in denial:

*The pornography doesn't really bother me, it's only pictures.*

*If I were more attractive he would not be doing this.*

*She can't help it if other men throw themselves at her.*

*Work must be his problem; if he would just change jobs.*

*If we move away from this neighborhood, she will stop this behavior.*

Denial is understandable. You deny because you want to trust your partner and believe that what he or she tells you is true. You want to believe that your values about commitment are shared. Yet you find yourself chronically giving him or her the benefit of the doubt despite your own intuition or suspicions telling you otherwise. The consequence to this is that you lose yourself in this process by failing to see your partner for who he or she is and by quieting your voice. Instead, you see him or her through rose-colored glasses, because they reflect how you want and need him or her to be. Confused by self-deception, you do not take action. You spend your energy reacting or stamping out fires. Denial is the oxygen feeding the fire.

Tapping into the truth ignites your greatest fear: Owning your truth and speaking it will lead to thoughts that tell you that you are not loved, not worthy, and the relationship may end. You feel shame and humiliation at not being able to confront your fears or change how you are being treated by the addict. So long as your partner denies, particularly when you don't have proof, the illusion of safety and security remains intact, once again reigniting the belief that all is well in the relationship and quieting those fears you wish to suppress.

Often there are clear indicators that a serious problem exists, but you may not see it or pointedly decide to ignore it. Facing the indicators accelerates all the fears that bubble to the surface of your mind. What does it mean if you find out he's lying? More arguing? Disrupting the children's lives? Lifestyle is threatened? You are not desirable? There's someone else who gets his time and affection? Punishment from the church? While you are busy questioning yourself, the addict stands strong and walled off, denying, protecting his or her stash and secret life, and continuing the addiction. A separate, yet mutual form of denial takes hold within the relationship.

Be compassionate with yourself and understand that you did not willfully get to this place of lying to yourself. While your denial has likely enabled hurtful behaviors to spiral out of control, denial in and of itself can have both pros and cons.

**Pro**: Denial helps to protect from the overwhelming pain of reality you might be facing. Denial can serve as a means to allow reality to come in smaller doses rather than all at once. For example, when you are about to set out on a grueling feat such as a marathon, or saving money for a high-ticket item, you discount the sacrifice, you discount the physical wear and tear, and the amount of time and effort involved and only see the end result. But addiction has a life of its own. Your partner's behavior was not just an incident or an act; it became compulsive. Once it began, the behavior couldn't just be brought to a close—it had become addictive.

**Con**: The risk you run in not facing denial means things stay the same or get worse. It means your reality and trust remain with the addict—you give up your own power.

- What do you think you gained from going into and maintaining denial?

- What have you lost by maintaining denial?

Overcoming your denial means deciding to face the truth about your circumstances. This is not an easy choice, but is a necessary one in creating a meaningful plan to manage the fallout of what has occurred. Part of facing the truth means experiencing the pain and confronting the fears that you sought to avoid. When denial is diminished, pain and fear often become overwhelming, and you spiral into another round of denial, landing you squarely back into the place you began. Recovery can be a roller coaster; there can be three steps forward and then one back, then three forward again. So again, be kind to yourself. This is hard; you are in a process in which emotions clearly override rational thinking. Your job is simply to be as honest with yourself as you possibly can be.

- What are the fears, thoughts, and behaviors that make it hard to confront your denial?

- Part of the goal now is to look beyond the fears and take an honest appraisal as to what you might gain by confronting your denial. What could you gain if you face your denial?

Without denial, the pain may seem even deeper. But you are ready to live in reality knowing you have the strength to move forward. The tools will keep coming; the support is here. Take a moment to acknowledge the important work you have just completed. Do some deep breathing or take a walk. Find a way to nurture yourself.

## Protecting the Illusion

*This section will guide you to be more specific about your denial system, recognizing how you have minimized and rationalized. This acknowledgment is critical to being able to identify your use of these defenses in the present. While the defenses are most likely well-developed, it will take vigilant awareness on your part to diminish them.*

Denial is the king, the granddaddy defense strategy to avoid reality, but it is fueled by another defense strategy: rationalizing. Rationalizing is a form of irrational thinking where you tell yourself the behavior of the addict can be explained in a way that makes it acceptable. You think your way through it while deflecting and avoiding the feelings associated with the thoughts.

Below are examples of rationalizing. Write down all that apply to you.

- Men will be men.

- She is an honest person; she would not lie to me.

- The lipstick on his collar got there when a coworker asked him to dance— he didn't want to be rude and say no.

- He's not really staring at women; he's just interested in watching people.

- He's not flirting, that's just his nature; he's a very friendly guy.

- We took vows before God. He would not break his vows.

- He is such a religious man and he takes his faith seriously.

- It doesn't hurt to look at pictures (porn); at least he is not having an affair.

- It's just easier for her to be friends with men; it doesn't mean she is having an affair.

- His business calls him away. After all, he does it so the kids and I can have a good lifestyle.

- Her business takes priority over the kids and me, but I understand. It's just while she is building her career.

- It's important for him to go to business functions without me. I'm not comfortable there, and I have to take care of the kids anyway.

- I must have gotten this STD from a toilet seat. He told me I couldn't have gotten it from him.

- Just because they have lunch together doesn't mean they are having an affair. He has to do business with her.

- She told me the long distance calls were not hers. The phone company must have made a mistake.

- It's okay if he gives her a Christmas gift. After all, she does work for him.

- Those Internet spammers are infiltrating our email with porn sites.

- The police are exaggerating about his behavior.

- I bet the babysitter called these telephone sex numbers when she was here.

- This is the way he grew up.

- She's such a good mother.

- It's not his fault that I can't fulfill him sexually.

- I am the one he comes home to.

When rationalizations aren't enough, minimization is the next strategy called in. That only strengthens the denial. It also serves to delay decisions, actions, or facing feelings by lessening the importance of the situation. In this way you can deceive yourself into thinking that your pain is "not that bad."

The following are minimizations common to those in relationships with sex addicts. Write down those that you have used and any others that are uniquely yours.

- It's not that bad.

- I pretend my relationship is strong when in fact I am very lonely.

- I'm the only one who really understands him.

- She needs me—now more than ever.

- It's just a phase.

- It's not his fault that whore went after him; he didn't have a chance.

- She's so great in all other areas, it's just this one area.

- I'm not that interested in sex anyway.

- It could be worse. At least he or she is not addicted to _____ (something other than sex, e.g., alcohol, other drugs, gambling, shopping, etc.)

- It doesn't matter if I don't know everything he does.

As you think about the ways in which you protected the illusion of the relationship, consider the thoughts and feelings that bolstered your denial.

For the statements below, write down all that apply to you. Next to each, write the feeling that emerges for you.

- I can't live without him or her.

- I might end up alone, and if I am alone that proves I am not worthy.

- No one else will ever love me.

- I don't deserve any better.

- He's the father of my children, and they need their father.

- All men/women are like this.

- I would have to give up some of my lifestyle because there is not enough money.

- My family might find out and I'd feel humiliated.

- The kids might find out and I won't know how to handle it.

- I might have to give up my home.

- I've never balanced a checkbook, paid bills, or paid attention to our retirement, and I am not capable.

- If others found out about his or her sexual behavior they would think I'm not a good sexual partner, because if I were, he or she would not stray.

- If he or she is a sex addict, then all the good times we had in the past were a lie.

It can be helpful to make this even more personal by doing the following exercise.

- Thinking back to when you met until present day, begin to note the times and/or situations when you suspected, saw, heard, or became aware of your partner's sexual acting out. Then note what you told yourself to minimize, rationalize, or blatantly deny the reality. Spend time on this exercise and come up with as many examples as you can.

EXAMPLES

| What I suspected, saw, heard, or knew about the sexual acting out. | How I minimized, denied, and/or rationalized it. |
| --- | --- |
| While we were dating I found out he had resumed contact with his ex-girlfriend and had lied about doing it. | I told myself he just needed that last fling. I wanted to believe I was important enough to him that it was just a one-time mistake. He apologized and seemed sincere. |
| I knew that just weeks before our wedding, when she went out with some of her friends, that she slept with another man. | I told myself that this would be her last time, and now she is mine forever. I thought this was just something women did prior to their weddings. |
| He was picked up for exhibitionism. | I told myself the humiliation would stop this type of behavior. |
| I was pregnant with our third child when I became aware he was frequently messing around on me. | I told myself the constant pregnancies pushed him away from me, and I wasn't physically desirable. That I would have a tubal ligation and get back in shape, and he wouldn't do that anymore. |

The purpose in doing this is to help you recognize denial and rationalizing. You can become so adept at it that you automatically go there unless you have developed the skills to recognize it. It is in recognizing these defenses that you have the potential to stop accepting the unacceptable, distorting reality, or partaking in deception. The truth is hard, but when you stand in the face of the truth, you are empowered in your choices.

## Cloudy to Clear: Transforming Distorted Thinking

*Here we will present nine types of faulty thinking patterns that go beyond rationalizing and minimizing. It is another exercise in becoming more cognizant of your own unhealthy thinking patterns and learning how to counter them.*

When living with deception and uncertainty it is only natural to engage in distorted thinking. Being confused, doubtful of self, frightened, and angry fuels the inability to think clearly. You've already looked at ways you've rationalized, minimized, or denied, which are all examples of distorted thinking. This exercise will allow you to identify other styles of thinking that add to the chaos and drama of what is happening in your life.

## STYLES OF DISTORTED THINKING

| | |
|---|---|
| **Filtering** | Looking at only one part of a situation to the exclusion of everything else. |
| **Polarized Thinking** | Perceiving everything at the extremes, all-or-nothing thinking with no middle ground. |
| **Overgeneralization** | Reaching a broad generalized conclusion based on just one piece of evidence. |
| **Mind Reading** | Making assumptions and reaching conclusions based on what you believe others are thinking. |
| **Catastrophizing** | Always expecting the worst-case scenario. |
| **Personalization** | Interpreting everything around you in a way that reflects on you and your self-worth. |
| **Change Fallacy** | Assuming that other people will change to suit you if you pressure them enough. |
| **Blaming** | Believing that bad, hurtful things that happen are someone else's fault. |
| **Shoulds** | Operating from a rigid set of indisputable rules about how everyone, including you, should act. |

Identify examples of when you engaged in distorted ways of thinking. List the examples you give that you believe you engage in frequently.

EXAMPLES

**Filtering**: *He tells me he had thoughts about another woman and I begin to search through his emails looking for evidence he is acting out. I ignore his telling me that he's reported this to his sponsor and has increased his number of meetings.*

**Polarized**: *When I feel good about her, I love her and could never doubt her. When I catch her lying, I hate her and never want to see her again.*

**Overgeneralization**: *I heard him speaking to a woman on the phone. I'm sure he's seeing prostitutes again.*

**Mind Reading**: *When I walk into his workplace, I know his coworkers must be thinking that I'm a fool for staying after they heard what he was doing.*

**Catastrophizing**: *He is being sued for sexual harassment, which means he won't be able to work in his field again, and we will lose the house and never be able to own one again.*

**Personalization**: *I just know her having an affair is because I am not a strong person.*

**Change Fallacy**: *I keep thinking if I become sexier he won't want those other women.*

**Blaming**: *I know the women he works with make it impossible for him to stay in recovery.*

**Shoulds**: *I should be more trusting.*

• Now think of a counter thought for each of the examples you gave.

EXAMPLES

**Filtering Counter Thought**: *He tells me he had thoughts about another woman, and while I feel angry and scared, I realize he is telling me his thoughts so as not to have any secrets, and that comes from his trying to practice recovery.*

**Polarized Counter Thought**: *When I feel good about her I need to accept that I have the right to feel good, but that doesn't mean everything is forever okay; and vice versa, when I am angry that doesn't mean I throw out the baby with the bathwater. I just take it a moment at a time.*

**Overgeneralization Counter Thought**: *Just because I overhear him talking to another woman doesn't mean he's acting out, but I will ask him who he was talking to.*

**Mind Reading Counter Thought**: *When I walk into his workplace I have no idea what the people who look at me are thinking or what they even know. I cannot afford to get caught up in trying to guess their thoughts.*

**Catastrophizing Counter Thought**: *He is being sued and right now we don't know what that means for us financially. I will attend the meetings with the attorneys and stay informed.*

**Personalization Counter Thought**: *I must maintain boundaries and remember her behavior isn't a statement about me, and vice versa.*

**Change Fallacy Counter Thought**: *It is not my job to change another person, nor do I have the power to do that.*

**Blaming Counter Thought**: *It doesn't help me to focus on others. I need to be accountable for me.*

**Shoulds Counter Thought**: *I can hear myself saying "I should" and that only gets me in trouble. I don't necessarily have any reason to be more trusting.*

It is important to be able to name the styles of thinking that sabotage your healing and to be aware when you are engaging in such thoughts. When you find yourself there, tell yourself to STOP, and immediately offer yourself a counter thought. This takes practice, but with practice your thinking will become much clearer. Remember, you don't need to do this alone—allowing others to provide feedback and support is helpful in learning new behaviors.

Identifying and countering distorted thinking neutralizes self-defeating thoughts, making it possible to cope with reality in a healthier manner.

## Magical Thinking: Challenging the Fantasy

*Magical thinking is an aspect of denial—projecting or living in a false image. This exercise challenges you to think about the degree to which you live in fantasy, how you work at image management and use your perfectionism to uphold the fairy tale.*

When confronting the various ways your distorted thinking protects you from facing reality, it's very likely you will recognize that aspects of your relationship have been based in the fantasy about who your partner was and what the relationship was about. In the absence of honest communication, you developed a relationship with an illusion. The illusion being, "all is okay in this relationship; I am loved and respected; and he or she would never leave me."

### EXAMPLES

*I liked our lifestyle and our friends. I loved him and believed he loved me. So I just kept up the pretense, the image, because to do anything differently would make me question what this meant about me.*

. . . .

*How could I not act like everything was okay? How could I say to people that my life and my marriage were a farce, a lie? They probably knew, but what did that say about me? I'm a fool? To allow myself to realize I was no different than his previous two wives was humbling when I had been so smitten.*

A lot hinges on your belief that all is okay. Your relationship, your family, possibly your livelihood, and certainly your self-esteem are at stake. To let go of the fantasy may mean letting go of the stability as you perceive it. But it is a fantasy based on illusion since it inadequately reflects parts of the relationship and not the whole itself. Being financially secure or emotionally safe doesn't match up with a person who also belittles you and goes elsewhere for sexual gratification. Paradoxically, it is when you relinquish the fantasy that you make room for growth and healing to occur. It means stepping into the abyss, the space of not knowing. Facing the unknown is scary. But your recovery work offers you a path, a direction, and a reason to be hopeful. All of that makes it easier to confront those fears and pretenses that bind you.

- Do you think you have engaged in fantasy about your relationship? If so, give at least three examples of how you engaged in fantasy.

- Have you been acting as if everything is fine when in reality you know on some level you are in fact not fine? Describe.

- Do you identify with attempting to project an image of a strong, healthy marriage when in fact it's been in grave trouble? Is the fantasy something you are willing to give up?

- What do you lose and/or what do you gain by letting go of the fantasy? Write down at least three examples of each.

Acknowledging and owning your magical thinking will make it possible to recognize how fantasy has served to protect you from your fears. You are developing skills to address those fears and will no longer use fantasy to protect the reality. The fact that you are working the exercises in this book demonstrates a willingness to face the truth. This takes courage. Reality is often hard to face. Know you are not in this alone. There are others able to walk side-by-side with you.

## Stepping Out of the Victim Role

*This section will help you acknowledge the victim role within betrayal and challenge you to take ownership for how you want to live your life today. It will help you make choices to explore how not to be victimized further. While you cannot change the behaviors of others, you can change how you think and respond.*

Owning your victimization means recognizing that you've been betrayed. You have placed trust in your partner; you trusted him or her to be honest, to honor his or her commitment, and then found your trust was violated. As overwhelming as is betrayal and its aftermath, a part of recovery is knowing when recycling the old hurts and wounds is keeping you further victimized—only now by yourself and not the actions of the addict.

To move out of being a victim you must own your reality and create emotional and physical safety for yourself. Going forward and challenging the dynamics of being powerless over what was done to you means taking a stance on how you want to live your life today. Getting unstuck from the effect of the addict's actions means making choices to explore how not to be victimized any further. While you cannot change the addict, you do have the power to change how you think and respond.

In an earlier section of this book you explored the role of victimization as a trauma response to your partner's sexual acting out. In this exercise you will work to recognize

1.) when you are engaged in victim thinking;

2.) how it's manifested behaviorally; and

3.) what to do about it.

Essential to moving out of the victim role is recognizing when your thinking is fostering tolerance for inappropriate behavior. To recognize when this is occurring you need to identify common forms of victim thinking and behaviors.

The following are common beliefs that fuel victimization. Write down all those that apply to you.

- My feelings and thoughts aren't important.
- This is futile; I can't do anything about it.
- I deserve(d) this.
- Other people are more important than me.
- I have no power.
- No one will believe me.
- I am stupid.

- List any other statements that reflect what you think when you're feeling victimized.

There are many ways these beliefs get acted out. The following are common behaviors that are manifested when you operate from victim thinking.

- **Helpless position:** Acting from the belief you have no power to act.

- **Chronic apologizer:** Acting from the belief you are always at fault, always responsible, yet have no power.

- **Dependent:** Believing if you say something he or she will leave and that you have no value without him or her.

- **Resentful:** Holding onto feelings of unspoken anger and silently seething. Feeling powerless to change things.

- **Complainer:** Sidestepping the real issue and complaining a lot about the unimportant things.

As painful as your experience is, awareness and sensitivity to being hurt can result in greater self-protection. Beginning to challenge a different outcome starts with believing you don't deserve to be treated badly or disrespectfully. It means honoring yourself and your rights.

## BILL OF RIGHTS

You have the right to be you.

You have the right to be safe.

You have the right to be treated with respect.

You have the right to put yourself first.

You have the right to make decisions that affect you.

You have the right to say no.

You have the right to make mistakes.

You have the right to ask questions about anything that affects your life.

You have the right to not be responsible for other adults' problems.

You have the right to earn and control your own money.

You have the right to be human, not perfect.

You have the right to be angry and protest if you are treated unfairly or abusively by anyone.

You have the right to not be liked by everyone.

You have the right to love and be loved.

While all rights are critically important, write down the rights from the Bill of Rights you need to pay particular attention to and add any additional ones that are important to you.

Trying out new behaviors may at first feel uncomfortable, but with support, validation, and repeated efforts, you'll get stronger in your ability to challenge the old ways that have hurt you. In your journal, copy the three column headers below and write in your own examples.

EXAMPLES

| How were you mistreated, ignored, or disrespected by your partner? | What did you think or do in response? | What could you tell yourself that would support you in taking healthier actions? |
|---|---|---|
| He was critical of my weight. | I felt I was not good enough, pretty enough, or sexy enough for him. | I can tell myself that I am attractive and that I am enough. |
| He would come home late and tell me he'd gone to a strip club. | I thought I was being a loving wife by accepting his needs. I thought his going to strip clubs was what men do and as long as he wasn't having an affair, what harm could it do? *I was afraid of losing him and thought giving him what he wanted would make him never leave me.* | I can write and read my affirmations. I will hold on to my boundaries, which allow me my self-respect. I can communicate my thoughts and what I need directly to him. |

Changing your view of being a victim takes practice and resolve. Those closest to you and used to you the old way may fight those changes. However, coming to terms with ending your victimization and asserting your rights means you become a stronger and more capable person worthy of love, attention, and respect.

## Tolerating the Intolerable

*Now we will help you identify the many times you have tolerated hurtful or inappropriate behavior. It is essential to recognize, identify, and own this tolerance to be able to stop engaging in the behavior and become more honest about your feelings. You will be introduced to thinking about new, more constructive, and certainly more empowering responses to the painful behaviors that you have passively endured.*

One of the hazards of living in a relationship where addiction exists is prolonged exposure to inappropriate and devaluing behavior. When subjected to hurtful and inappropriate behavior over time, people learn to react submissively, often allowing themselves to become victimized in the process. By allowing unacceptable behaviors to continue without recognizing healthier options and choices in how to respond, you become complicit in a cycle of abuse and neglect that is hard to stop until a crisis occurs that forces you to reevaluate your role. Betrayed partners often have come from relationships where these patterns of submission and victimization existed, frequently denying or not knowing how they felt. This allowed them, unwittingly, to be further mistreated.

What results is a lot of confusion and helplessness, and a high tolerance for hurtful and neglectful behavior. Too often when you've attempted to express your concern or your feelings, your partner responded in a defensive or avoidant way. You were given the cold shoulder or somehow you were made to feel wrong or bad for having voiced a concern. That resulted in the message to yourself of "Why bother? Nothing good will come from this." For example, your partner makes a sexual remark to a waitress. The comment is out-of-the-blue and inappropriate. You feel embarrassed, but tell yourself it's better not to say anything because he would just become loud and defensive and more people would become aware of his inappropriateness. While in the moment that may be a good judgment call on your part, this situation is never confronted. You have just instated the "don't talk," "don't feel" rules. In this process, there is a chronic eroding of your own esteem.

When such occurrences happen repeatedly over time, you develop a high tolerance for inappropriate behavior. Many partners get to a point wherein they are numb and no longer recognize the inappropriateness. These patterns are often learned in childhood. If you were raised in an addictive or abusive home it is likely you came into this relationship with skills that reinforced not having your needs met or even knowing what needs are, thereby rationalizing them away. This high tolerance, which may have its foundation in your childhood experiences, is fueled by the degree to which you 1) saw and believed it was safer to avoid conflict, 2) are fearful of rejection and abandonment, and 3) have a strong need for another's approval.

Recognizing situations in which you tolerate inappropriate behavior means identifying and naming the intrusive, offending behavior. Ending your victimization begins with you and takes time. It starts with situations, small or large, where you can begin to say, "No, I am not okay with this." Some partners when they first learned of the betrayals were able to say, "This is unacceptable and you have to leave the home and live elsewhere." Taking this form of action is often the turning point from old ways of tolerating unacceptable behaviors to new ways of respecting self with appropriate limit-setting.

Identify times in which you felt your partner's behavior was hurtful or inappropriate and you said nothing or pretended as though it had not occurred. What were the feelings you had at the time?

**EXAMPLES**

*My wife told me she had to work long hours as a means to further her career. I accepted this for many years, never challenging it. Now I know that her schedule allowed her to meet with her lovers because she never had a schedule to be at home except when she wanted to. Feeling: fearful.*

· · · ·

*Money was missing from the checking account and my husband told me that it was his business since he earned the money. I never challenged it and later I learned that he was funding escorts right in front of my eyes. Feeling: hurt/angry.*

· · · ·

*I caught him in a lie and acted like I didn't notice. Feeling: fearful.*

- With each example you gave, describe some of the justifications or rationalizations you made to yourself in order for it to be okay.

The way to stop this behavior is to be able to recognize it is occurring. When you are in an uncomfortable situation where a high-tolerance response is common for you, ask yourself the following questions:

- Is this behavior okay with me? Why or why not?

- Is this behavior respectful of me and my feelings?

- How do I feel about this?

We suggest that you use your journal on a daily basis to identify anything that you tolerated that was inappropriate, the feelings associated, and then create an alternative response.

### EXAMPLES

**Tolerated Inappropriate Behavior:**
*He blatantly flirted with my daughter's friend and I said nothing.*

**Feeling or Attitude:**
*Angry, horrified*

**Alternative Behavior:**
*I could have said it was not okay to say such things to our daughter's friend, in fact to any woman other than me and that he needed to apologize to both our daughter and her friend.*

• • • •

**Tolerated Inappropriate Behavior:**
*I caught her in a lie and acted like I didn't know it.*

**Feeling or Attitude:**
*Afraid*

**Alternative Behavior:**
*I could tell her that I knew she was not where she said she was.*

Becoming aware of high-tolerance is a process. You are more likely to increase your awareness of how accommodating or tolerant you are over time. Recognizing the ways this occurs is a huge step in changing the patterns. Speaking to others about how you see the situation is a good way to get a reality check as to whether your reaction is demonstrating high-tolerance or not.

List those people you will contact for this reality check.

By using the tools previously outlined, you become a greater participant in the direction you want your life to take. You also break the pattern of allowing others to take advantage of you. Relationships become more mutually beneficial and reciprocal and intimate connections flourish.

# C: Psychological Challenges

## My Risky Behaviors

*This section offers you a way to look at the possibility of engaging in your own high-risk behaviors, such as sexual acting out, unhealthy eating, spending money or gambling excessively, and/or use of alcohol or other drugs. If you realize you may be struggling with any of these issues, it is important to get honest and address them or any recovery that is related to the sexual betrayal will be severely impeded.*

Although much of your attention has been focused on your partner's sexual addiction, the next exercise is meant to help you explore areas in yourself where imbalance and perhaps addictive patterns exist. It is not uncommon that as a response to stress and/or as a means to manage intolerable feelings, a betrayed partner finds him- or herself engaging in and depending upon addictive behaviors. Whether it is a substance addiction found in the use of alcohol or other drugs, or certain process behaviors like shopping, love and relationship addiction, or an eating disorder, you may find yourself relying more and more on the use of these manifestations to help you cope with the stress of the betrayal. The behaviors may have preceded the sexual addiction or they may be an adaptive response to the crisis. What often begins in innocence can unknowingly become a maladaptive means to manage life's uncertainties.

### LOVE AND RELATIONSHIP ADDICTION

Love and relationship addiction is characterized by a fear of abandonment and rejection stemming from a childhood where emotional needs were inconsistently met, or for some, not met at all. Love and relationship addicted patterns are shaped by an underlying belief that your worth and value is measured through your relationship to a partner, regardless of how he or she treats you. Consider the following signs that love and relationship addiction may be present:

- Confusing love with intensity and/or frequency of sex.

- Having a history of destructive relationships where attempts to end the relationship often failed. Fights and threats to leave or be left result in high stress and drama.

- A history of being with partners who are unavailable and/or highly controlling.

- Being without a partner is terrifying and something to avoid at all costs. Underlying this pattern is the belief that your worth and value only exists within the context of a relationship.

- Compromising values in order to secure or keep a relationship.

- Lacking boundaries. Not being able to say no when you want to, "I don't know how to stick up for myself, to set a boundary."

- Difficulty ending relationships despite the emotional or physical toll on you.

- Intimacy is false, fleeting, based in fantasy and magical thinking.

- Rushing into another relationship prematurely; often having a new potential partner waiting in the wings.

- Living in fear the relationship could end at any time. Thoughts such as "he or she could leave at any time." "I am not good enough."

- Fantasy, intensity, and romance result in distortions of reality.

- Engaging in high-risk sexual behaviors often resulting in sexually transmitted diseases and unplanned pregnancies and/or abortions. The risk taking is often out of fear of losing the relationship.

## ADDICTIVE DISORDERS

While love and relationship addiction is more prevalent, other common process addictions are gambling and spending. Eating disorders like compulsive overeating, anorexia, and bulimia are different expressions of the pain you are experiencing. You may also need to look at your own sexual behaviors. It is not uncommon that both people within a relationship are sexually addicted. The prevalent addiction in our Western culture is that of substance addiction. You may be struggling with your own use of alcohol and/or other drugs, such as prescription pain pills.

In your wildest dreams you didn't see yourself losing the ability to control your own behavior. Yet your drug/behavior of choice does something nothing else has been able to—it takes away the pain, provides temporary relief, and offers a sense of control. Addiction is a pathological relationship with a mood-altering substance or behavior that you continue despite the fact that it creates adverse consequences in significant areas of your life.

A simple way to think about whether or not something is a problem for you is using the acronym of SAFE:

- **S** stands for secretive. Is the behavior, the substance, the frequency, or the amount in which you engage something others are not aware of? Is it something you do not want to discuss openly? You may think it is not a secret, but in fact, if you find you're not being open about the degree to which you spend time engaging in or are preoccupied with it, then it is secretive.

- **A** stands for abusive. Is the behavior or substances hurtful or harmful to yourself or another at this stage? Is it hurting your relationship with someone else even if he or she is unaware? Is it harming you in some way, keeping you away from other priorities? Is it harmful to your self-esteem? Your finances? Your health?

- **F** stands for feelings. Does this process or behavior separate or remove you from your feelings? Does it medicate your feelings? Or is it the only time in which you experience feelings?

- **E** stands for emptiness. After you have engaged in this process or behavior for some time, does it now leave you with a sense of emptiness? Do you find yourself reengaging more quickly than you have in the past—leading to another **E**, which is escalation.

People can be addicted to just about anything, ranging from exercise, to gambling, to spending money, shopping, another person, or a substance. But it is not the act itself that is the problem. The problem is the compulsion to keep doing it excessively or recklessly. Going shopping is fun; it's when it leads you into debt and destroys your family that it becomes a problem. One drink may be fine; it's when it becomes multiple drinks and results in avoiding your responsibilities or making decisions you regret that it becomes a problem.

It is important to understand that being addicted is not a statement about your worth and value. Nor is it a statement about your strength or willpower. Addiction can happen to anybody. Becoming addicted has a lot to do with issues such as biological vulnerability, emotional pain, trauma histories, belief systems, and social modeling.

We live in a quick-fix, feel-good culture that reinforces seeking outside answers to inside problems. We all need escape mechanisms. It is when we come to rely on our escape behavior to relieve our sense of unworthiness that it becomes compulsive in nature. The compulsive aspect of this process or behavior then becomes central to our lives, creating distance between us and others, separating us from our inner truth, and interfering with our ability to be honest with ourselves.

From the list below, write down all that may be a concern or problem for you.

**Substances**

- Alcohol
- Amphetamines (e.g., speed, diet pills)
- Marijuana
- Cocaine
- Hallucinogens (e.g., Ecstasy, LSD, mushrooms)
- Inhalants (e.g., glue, paint)
- Opioids (e.g., heroin, morphine, methadone)
- Sedatives (e.g., sleeping pills, tranquilizers)
- Nicotine (e.g., smoking)
- Food (compulsive overeating)
- Other

**Processes**

- Gambling
- Internet
- Food (anorexia, bulimia)
- Sex
- Love/relationship
- Exercise
- TV
- Shopping/spending money
- Work
- Hoarding
- Shoplifting
- Cosmetic surgery
- Other

- Noting the concerns you wrote down, describe any of the consequences that you see affecting the following areas:

  - **Relationship problems**: These may include not being there for family/friends due to your behavior; people expressing concern about your use; isolating; inappropriate or hurtful behavior directed toward family/friends; or spending time with dangerous people. Describe the relationship problems you notice.

  - **Legal problems**: These may include using that results in driving under the influence; loss of custody of children; arrest; or illegal behavior. Describe the legal problems you notice.

- **Physical problems**: These may include using that results in unsafe sex; a worsening medical condition such as diabetes or infection; or neglecting your body. Describe the physical problems you notice.

- **Emotional problems**: These may include using that results in depression, anxiety, or unhealthy anger; wanting to hurt yourself or others; low self-esteem; guilt; or shame. Describe the emotional problems you notice.

- **Work problems**: These may include using that results in being fired, missing work, or poor performance. Describe the work problems you notice.

- With each possible manifestation of addiction that you noted for yourself, to what degree are you concerned?

- Name the behavior and whether you are

  Not concerned

  A little concerned

  Moderately concerned

  Extremely concerned

- How much of an addiction problem do you feel you have? Do you believe it's

  No problem

  A little problem

  Moderate problem

  Extreme problem

If you responded with either "moderate" or "extreme" on either question, would you be willing to

- Discuss this with a helping professional

- Attend a twelve-step group

- Read literature about a specific manifestation of addiction

- Other

It takes courage to explore the possibility of addiction in your own life, but your willingness to do so is also a statement about your commitment to *your* healing. You will find information about twelve-step programs and suggested readings in the Resources section. We also suggest if you are presently working with a counselor, you let him or her know the area(s) about which you are concerned. Acknowledging that you are struggling with a possible manifestation of addiction doesn't take away from what has been occurring in your relationship, but attending to it will give you the foundation to move forward in your healing from the sexual betrayals and deception.

## Other Emotional Concerns

*The fact that you may not only be engaging in risky behaviors, but experiencing anxiety and/or depression, may warrant professional treatment. There are many different forms of depression and anxiety, and this section will give you a brief overview of each, offering you an opportunity to be more informed and to determine whether or not any of the thinking or behavior you have been experiencing is influenced by one or more of these disorders.*

The longer you have lived with untreated addiction the more likely you are to experience problems with regulating emotions. Depending upon the degree of trauma in your background, the greater the effects will be to your mental health. As you engage in recovery you will be able to differentiate symptoms, which, although exacerbated as a result of this crisis in your life, may have preceded the crisis and may be inhibiting you in moving forward. This can be a sign that a second, or co-occurring, problem exists. Emotional disorders are treatable and it's important to address them to create further opportunity for you to be successful in your recovery.

### DEPRESSIVE DISORDERS

**Major Depression**: Characterized by feelings of sadness and irritability that interfere with daily living. There is no exact cause of depression, but many who study depression believe it is caused by chemical changes in the brain. Biological predisposition, psychological injury, and chronic stress can lead to depression. Depression is also a learned behavior that influences your thinking. A household where children are exposed to adverse experiences can result in faulty, pessimistic thinking leading to self-defeating thoughts—also key symptoms of depression. Unresolved grief, that is, having many losses that are not addressed when they occur and are left untreated, becomes a negative coping mechanism enabling one to avoid facing present day challenges or losses. Faced with the grief related to the many losses of living with sex addiction, you may now be compelled to address this underlying disorder: depression. There are degrees to which someone can be affected by depression, but by far the most debilitating and life-threatening is major depressive disorder.

Symptoms of major depression:

- Depressed mood most of the day; feeling sad or empty, tearful.
- Significant loss of interest or pleasure in activities that used to be enjoyable.
- Difficulty sleeping or sleeping too much.
- Fatigue or loss of energy.
- Poor concentration or having difficulty making decisions.
- Significant weight loss (when not dieting) or weight gain; decrease or increase in appetite.
- Agitation; or slowing of thoughts and reduction of physical movements.
- Thoughts about death or suicide.

**Dysthymia:** Persistent mild depression lasting on and off for a period of six months to two years. A person with dysthymia experiences many of the same symptoms as the person with major depression without the suicidal thoughts. They also have a higher level of daily functioning. The dysthymic person often reports an absence of joy in all areas of life, as if life is dulled. The negative affect of dysthymia is less visible to the world as the person with this type of depression may be good at hiding his or her internal despair and self-loathing from others, so others are less likely to notice it.

Dysthymic symptoms include:

- Loss of interest in daily activities.
- Feeling sad, empty, or down.
- Lack of energy.
- Trouble concentrating.
- Trouble making decisions.
- Self-criticism.
- Decreased productivity.
- Feelings of guilt.

**Bipolar Disorder/Mania:** Characterized by extreme mood swings ranging from sadness and despair to racing thoughts and impulsive behaviors. There are different types of bipolar disorder that vary in frequency and duration. We advise against self-diagnosis, as this is a complex condition for which a consultation with a trained healthcare provider should be sought. When you live with someone who blatantly lies, tries to make you believe your thinking is crazy, and is skilled at these behaviors, it is common for your emotions to range from despair to rage, often at lightning speed. These symptoms can as likely be explained by the stress of your circumstances as much as they could also be an indicator of bipolar disorder, or both. Life stressors and family crises can trigger a cascade of symptoms resulting in a manic episode.

Signs of mania include:

- Decreased need for sleep.
- Racing thoughts.
- More talkative than usual; pressured speech.
- Rapidly changing, unrelated thoughts.
- Easily distracted.
- Driven behavior (at school, work, sexually).
- Risky behavior (e.g., excessive spending).
- Impulsive decision-making (e.g., quit job, marry, large financial purchases).
- Irritability.
- Poor judgment in social situations.
- Insomnia or need for less sleep.
- Beliefs of possessing exaggerated power, importance, knowledge, or ability.

## ANXIETY DISORDERS

**Generalized Anxiety Disorder (GAD):** Anxiety itself is a normal human emotion that everyone experiences at times. Many people feel anxious, or nervous, when faced with a problem at work, before taking a test, or making an important decision. Anxiety disorders, however, are different. They can cause such distress that it interferes with a person's ability to lead a normal life. This disorder involves excessive, unrealistic worry, and tension, even if there is little or nothing to provoke the anxiety. Generalized anxiety may also be an inherited condition exacerbated by the environment in which one was raised. Anxiety interferes with your life. You worry excessively and find yourself seeking constant reassurance from others only to find that doesn't help.

Generalized anxiety symptoms include:

- Restlessness or a feeling of being "keyed up" or "on edge."
- Being easily fatigued.
- Difficulty concentrating or a sense of your mind going blank.
- Irritability.
- Muscle tension.
- Difficulty sleeping.
- Trembling, twitching, muscle soreness.
- Headaches, sweating or chills, nausea, dizziness.
- Shortness of breath.
- Diarrhea.
- Irritable bowel syndrome.
- Being easily startled.

**Post-Traumatic Stress Disorder (PTSD):** A condition that can develop following a traumatic or terrifying event, such as a sexual or physical assault, the unexpected death of a loved one, or a natural disaster. People with PTSD often have lasting and frightening thoughts and memories of the event, and tend to be emotionally numb. Should you come from a history of family trauma and then, as an adult, experience traumas that are common to living with addiction, you may not have full blown PTSD, but you may nonetheless experience some of the symptoms of complex trauma.

Symptoms of trauma-related disorders include:

- Experiencing bad dreams or nightmares.
- Behaving or feeling as if specific situations were happening all over again (this is known as having flashbacks).
- Having a lot of emotional reactivity when you think about your situation.

- Having a lot of physical sensations when you think about your situation (e.g., your heart races or pounds; you sweat, find it hard to breathe, feel faint; or feel like you're going to lose control).

- Avoiding thoughts, conversations, or feelings that remind you about your situation.

- Avoiding people, places, or activities.

- Having difficulty remembering some important things in your life.

- Losing interest in, or just not doing things that used to be important to you.

- Feeling detached from people; finding it hard to trust people.

- Feeling emotionally "numb" and finding it hard to have loving feelings even toward those who are emotionally close to you.

- Having difficulty falling or staying asleep.

- Feeling irritable and having problems with anger.

- Having a hard time concentrating.

- Thinking you may not live much longer and feeling there's no point in planning for the future.

- Being jumpy and startling easily.

- Always "on guard."

It is not uncommon for partners to begin to experience other forms of anxiety disorder. Again, these may precede your relationship. The difficulty in your relationship may heighten the anxiety, or the anxiety may be fueled by your present life experiences.

**Panic Disorders:** A sudden surge of overwhelming anxiety and fear. In the midst of a panic attack, the physiological signs are so scary people often think they are dying. You may quickly end up in an emergency room clutching your chest only to be told you are physically fine—this is a panic attack, anxiety. In many cases, panic attacks strike out of the blue, without any warning. They may even occur when you're relaxed or asleep. A panic attack may be a one-time occurrence, but many people experience repeat episodes.

**Obsessive-Compulsive Disorder (OCD):** Constant thoughts or fears that cause those affected to perform certain rituals or routines. The disturbing thoughts are called obsessions, and the rituals are called compulsions. An example is a person with an unreasonable fear of germs (obsession) who constantly washes his or her hands (compulsion). If you have a history of OCD, the stress of your present-day situation most likely will escalate this disorder.

**Phobias:** A group of symptoms brought on by a fear of certain objects or situations. A specific phobia is a lasting and irrational fear caused by the presence or thought of a specific object or situation. Exposure to the object or situation brings about an immediate reaction even though it poses little or no actual danger, causing the person to endure intense anxiety (nervousness) or to avoid the object or situation entirely. The distress associated with the phobia and/or the need to avoid the object or situation can significantly interfere with the person's ability to function. Adults with a specific phobia recognize that the fear is excessive or unreasonable, yet are unable to overcome it.

There are different types of specific phobias, based on the object or situation feared, including animal phobias; situational phobias such as riding in a car or on public transportation, going over bridges or through tunnels, or being in a closed-in place; natural-environment phobias, such as the fear of storms or heights. A person can have more than one specific phobia.

**Social Phobia (also called social anxiety):** Overwhelming worry and self-consciousness about everyday social situations. The worry often centers on a fear of being judged by others or of behaving in a way that might cause embarrassment or lead to ridicule. Many partners avoid social events as they become increasingly aware of what is happening in their relationship. You want to hide because you feel as if you can't conceal the truth and that others can see right through you and are judging you.

While you may identify with many of the symptoms noted here—and not to minimize how horrific this may feel—the most relevant question as to whether or not this is a primary disorder would be "has this preceded the present crisis?" If these symptoms are mostly connected to your present crisis, it is very likely that as you allow yourself a forum in which to address what is happening in your life you will find these symptoms dissipating naturally. Should you have a history of social anxiety, it is likely your personal situation will fuel greater anxiety, and if so, professional evaluation for this anxiety should be sought.

**Attention Deficit/Hyperactivity Disorder (AD/HD):** A common behavioral disorder with symptoms that can be easily overlooked or that can be misdiagnosed. The most common features include distractibility (poor sustained attention to tasks), impulsivity (impaired impulse control and delay of gratification), and hyperactivity (excessive activity and physical restlessness).

In order to meet diagnostic criteria, these behaviors must be excessive, long-term, and pervasive. A crucial consideration is that the behaviors must create a real handicap in at least two areas of a person's life, such as school, home, work, or social settings. These symptoms are certainly accentuated if you have been living with sex addiction.

As you can see there is a lot of overlap to these disorders, and many of the symptoms are common to how you feel based on your situation. If you are diagnosed with one of these conditions, it is imperative you continue your recovery practice, as your codependency will only undermine any treatment of these conditions. If you believe you are experiencing any of the above conditions, we strongly encourage you to be assessed by a qualified medical professional or healthcare provider. A first step could be talking with your primary care physician, as he or she is often trained to screen and make referrals to more specialized providers. It is also imperative that you explain the symptoms you experienced when you learned about the addiction so that the consulting professional can put this into a proper context as to how to best treat your symptoms.

Be aware that the use of any mood-altering substances would only aggravate and mask symptoms of anxiety or depressive disorders. It is essential that if you think you have any of the above conditions that you seriously address your usage and certainly share honestly with the professional who is helping you.

If it is indicated that medication will help you, then consider this another tool necessary to aid you in your recovery—one that will enhance your quality of life, but like other tools in recovery, is not sustainable without a more holistic approach to self-care.

Are you concerned that you may be experiencing any of the above conditions? If so, describe your symptoms and concerns.

We think it is important to have offered you this information. If you are experiencing any of these problems, we encourage you to seek professional help for an evaluation. Starting with your primary care physician for a referral and recommendation is a good first step. Getting as much support as you can will help you move forward in your healing as you learn additional ways to regulate overwhelming emotions.

# CHAPTER FOUR

# Recognizing the Role of Childhood Influences

While you are attending to the immediate needs of your life there remains an underlying foundation that has done much to support your codependent and other unhealthy behaviors. To sustain long-term recovery it is necessary to look at the driving force behind your self-defeating thinking and behaviors. What you do in relationships today is often behavior learned in your growing-up years. The importance of recognizing this is to be able to identify carried beliefs and behaviors that no longer serve a purpose, and in fact, interfere with how you want to live your life. Exploring family influences is not about putting blame on your family or your parents. It is about beginning the process of putting the past behind you and creating new beliefs and behaviors that give you greater choices in your relational skills. It is important to look back at your early life and identify the critical experiences that shaped you. With that insight you'll want to ask to what degree you carry the lessons of those experiences into your present day relationship. This is a significant part to your healing. It will help you to define and give focus to your recovery.

## Generational Impact

*More people experience trauma within the confines of their family than situational trauma. Here you have the opportunity to look at whether or not you were influenced by forms of emotional and/or physical abandonment within your family. This will set the foundation for recognizing how you carry the influences of your original family system into your present-day relationships.*

So often when people think of trauma they think of acts of violence or terrorism or situations like an auto accident, a house fire, or a natural disaster such as a hurricane or an earthquake. But the majority of people who experience trauma experience it in the context of family.

Blatant forms of trauma within the family include being subjected to and/or witnessing physical and sexual abuse. Yet trauma can be even more subtle, such as living with fear on a chronic basis as a five-year-old, ten-year-old, even a fifteen-year-old, a vulnerable time in your life when you are trying to make sense of the world, developing beliefs about yourself and the world around you.

When you grow up in an environment that is traumatic to your development, it results in taking the vulnerability of who you were as a child into your adult life. Your pain, your losses, the inability to move through that pain, the defenses you created to cope, the faulty beliefs you developed about yourself and the world-at-large affect your relationships, parenting skills, work, and other aspects of your life.

People who have lived in less-than-nurturing environments learn to normalize their situations. With years of tolerating and accepting the way it was when you were growing up, it would be difficult to name your childhood experience as traumatic, since words such as traumatic or trauma sound harsh. But remember, you were a child, with the needs of a child and that means you needed to feel safe and secure with those who were supposed to nurture and care for you, your parents. So it is understandable that it may be difficult to name that which was hurtful in the past as hurtful.

Your family's job was to provide you with both roots and wings; roots to help you grow, develop, and flourish, and wings to help you leave home and develop a life and a family of your own. That is done by providing safety, security, and the environment in which to emotionally and mentally grow and flourish. First, by taking care of your physical needs, making sure you are fed appropriately and have clothing and shelter to protect you; next, ensuring that you are protected physically from harm, keeping you safe from hurtful people and seeing that normal childhood medical issues are attended to; and then attending to your educational needs and nurturing your school experience, seeing that you go to school, recognizing and attending to any special needs in that area. It is their role to direct you spiritually and to do this in a manner that offers guidance and respect for your individuality.

You need to feel and hear you are loved and are of value. Even more important than hearing words of love is having love demonstrated, such as with time and attention. Time is given through play and appropriate affection. Life needs to be predictable and consistent. Children need age-appropriate and realistic expectations. They need to be children. With healthy structure and clear communication, children learn not only to trust others but to trust themselves. Children learn communication skills from their parents. How to handle feelings, how to problem-solve, and how to resolve conflicts are skills taught predominantly through modeling.

As you enter into adulthood, you integrate all of these lessons into a sense of direction and purpose with the ability, through internalized values, to understand right from wrong, who is responsible for what, and what is meaningful in your life. Then you pursue that direction.

## GENERATIONAL INFLUENCES

Recognizing generational influences will help you identify your recovery needs. You do not have to be raised with addiction to partner with addiction as an adult. While many partners were raised in families where addiction occurred, you may also have experienced abuses or various forms of mental illness. Regardless of the source of dysfunction, the common denominator is loss—loss of nurturing and safety. Impairment in families occurs along a continuum. For some, loss is much more subtle, such as families where the parenting and relational styles are rigid or too permissive. Families that are highly enmeshed or those where there is severe relational disconnection also fuel codependent behaviors. While many partners strongly believe they were raised in healthy families, as they are confronted with their own unhealthy behaviors they come to recognize how aspects of their growing up years may be impacting their coping strategies today. This is not about blaming; this is about undoing denial and learning how to recognize reality.

## ABANDONMENT

While there is no such thing as perfect parenting, failure to meet your needs with consistency results in abandonment. There are two types of abandonment, physical and emotional. Physical abandonment means that your basic physical needs such as food, shelter, clothing, and appropriate supervision are not provided or attended to consistently. In addition to what is neglectful behavior on the part of your parents, physical abandonment may also be abuse—physical or sexual. If you were not given the protection, safety, and security you needed to thrive, you experienced abandonment.

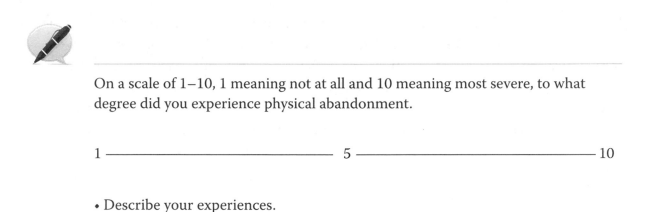

On a scale of 1–10, 1 meaning not at all and 10 meaning most severe, to what degree did you experience physical abandonment.

1 ———————————————— 5 ———————————————— 10

• Describe your experiences.

Emotional abandonment is when you have to hide a part of who you are in order to be acceptable and/or to protect yourself on a consistent basis. Examples of emotional abandonment you may have experienced from your primary caregiver(s)/parent(s) in your growing up years include being

- Criticized, compared to others, or otherwise belittled when you made a mistake.
  - The consequence is you learn to hide your mistakes/vulnerabilities from those closest to you.

- Punished or ridiculed when you expressed specific feelings.
  - The consequence is you learn to hide your feelings.

- Inconsistently attended to as a child.

  - The consequence is you have difficulty identifying and attaching value to your needs; your needs will only sometimes be met and are dependent on when the other person deems it so.

- Witness to your caregiver's/parents' bolstering their self-esteem by putting down people who have achieved greater accomplishments.

  - The consequence is that you learn to hide your accomplishments/successes; struggle with feelings of superiority/inferiority.

- Burdened with unrealistic expectations, expected to cope with and handle situations beyond your developmental age.

  - The consequence is that you learn fear of failure and either undercompensate or overcompensate to prove yourself.

- Attacked (verbally or physically) for your whole being, worth, and value versus what you did or did not do.

  - The consequence is that you think anything that disappoints another makes you unworthy and unlovable; difficulty separating your worth from your behavior.

- The vehicle for a parent's/caregiver's unfulfilled hopes and dreams without respect for your authenticity, your individual needs, your wishes and dreams.

  - The consequence is that you may live out another's future; believe you are responsible for others' thoughts, feelings, and actions; not feel free to live your own life.

- Treated as a peer rather than as a child.

  - The consequence is that you struggle and have confused relationship boundaries; lack a healthy distinction for expectations and roles within relationships; act falsely empowered with inward feelings of inadequacy.

Write down all of the ways you identify with any of these forms of emotional abandonment.

The greater the severity of the abandonment, the more it is disruptive to healthy self-esteem, a sense of worth and value, emotional maturity, and social and relational skills. Sadly, childhood abandonment sets you up to tolerate abandoning behavior in adult relationships. You are willing to dismiss your suspicions because after all, you don't want to do anything to him or her that would cause him or her to get angry with you. You will go to any length to avoid conflict, often discounting your own needs and wants in the process.

When your needs were not consistently met as you were growing up, you did not internalize your own sense of worth and value. The consequence is that you then seek outside validation in order to feel good about yourself. Without identifying and grieving the losses in your childhood you will continue the process of seeking your value and worth from the outside. That is when what has been traumatic to your development begins to repeat itself.

## Adult Repetition of Abandonment

*This section builds on the previous exercise, but asks you to look at the degree to which abandonment is repeated in your adult relationships. Even more important is the question, "In what ways do you abandon yourself?" In being able to answer that question you also tell yourself what you need to focus on to honor and respect yourself as you move forward in your life and recovery.*

Looking at the forms of abandonment that occurred in your childhood helps you to recognize similar experiences you may have in your relationships as an adult. But abandonment does not just exist in the context of what others do and don't do toward you. Ultimately, you must look at the possibility of how you abandon yourself.

### RELATIONSHIP ABANDONMENT

While forms of physical abandonment are most apparent in childhood, it certainly can occur in adult relationships when there is sexual infidelity and deception. The following examples represent present-day physical abandonment.

> EXAMPLES
>
> *Physical abandonment occurred in being exposed to STDs and not having my health respected.*

· · · ·

*Physical abandonment came in the form of being ignored sexually as my husband was caught up in his hours of cybersex.*

. . . .

*I experienced abandonment in the physical abuse of my wife's rages and her frequent absences.*

Looking at your most current relationship, how and to what degree have you experienced physical abandonment?

Emotional abandonment is even more pervasive than physical abandonment.

Examples of relationship abandonment would be when your partner

- Doesn't honor or acknowledge your needs or feelings;

- Lies and/or is not completely honest with you;

- Keeps secrets (lying by omission, what it is he or she isn't telling you);deflects, blames, and/or makes excuses rather than speaks to the behavior when confronted;

- Shows disrespect with name calling, blaming, etc.;

- Is critical of your performance in area of responsibilities, your appearance, social interactions, career;

- Finds reasons to justify acting out;

- Takes advantage of your goodwill, your efforts, taking from the relationship to fuel his or her addiction, for example, by taking time for family and putting it into the addiction.

Looking at your most current relationship, how and to what degree have you experienced emotional abandonment?

## SELF-ABANDONMENT

Sadly, the greatest act of abandonment is self-abandonment. When you experience abandonment as a child and abandonment in relationships, you have usually learned to abandon yourself.

Below are some examples of different ways you may abandon yourself.

- I expect perfection from myself. I am the first to berate/criticize myself for mistakes or vulnerabilities.

- I tell myself it is not okay to have certain feelings.

- I discount and minimize my own needs.

- I minimize my accomplishments/successes.

- I have unrealistic expectations of myself.

- When I am disappointed with myself, I attack my whole being, worth, and value versus what I did or did not do.

- I don't have boundaries that protect me.

What other ways do you abandon yourself? Complete the following sentence three times. This repetition often leads to greater insight.

*I have abandoned myself when I* _____.

While you will want to address any of the issues/challenges that interfere with your recovery, identify the ones most problematic at the moment and focus on those in your recovery work, be it with further reading, self-help groups, or counseling.

Your recovery needs to come first and, most importantly, should focus on no longer abandoning yourself. It is saying that you will engage in self-nurturing behavior and self-care, honoring and respecting yourself and that you will not tolerate hurtful behavior from others. This entails being able to recognize both self-abandonment and abandonment within the relationship. It is common that partners of sex addicts are more apt to begin the recovery process when the fear of losing self becomes greater than the fear of losing the relationship. When you accept responsibility for yourself and acknowledge and honor yourself, you will not get lost living in the shadow of someone else's behavior.

## Replaying the Past

*We now ask you to become more specific about patterns that are being repeated in your present-day relationship. This not only focuses on your most current relationship, but challenges you to look at your life-long pattern. By asking you to be specific, you have the opportunity to leave behind an old script and create a new vision and path.*

While it's likely you have carried traits from your childhood to the present, you may start recognizing that early childhood influences are taking a larger toll on your life than you imagined—the most apparent being that your relationship and relationship history replicates experiences you had growing up. Such a relationship—and in some cases there may be more than one relationship—is referred to as trauma repetition. This means you engage in behaviors and situations similar to those you experienced earlier in life. It means repeating a story that was scripted from your past. Replaying your past is often repeating what you know, the familiar, reinforced by underlying messages that reflect your beliefs about your self-worth. Often the outcome from childhood experiences left you wanting more of your parents' time and attention, or, alternatively, you became numb to even wanting to have your needs met. The problems you confront in adult relationships are often attempts to change the outcome of old family scripts.

### EXAMPLES

*My father had lots of affairs and my mother just acted like it wasn't happening. Well, now my husband has had a lot of affairs and I wasn't even aware. It is as if I am living my mother's life all over. As a kid I learned not to trust my gut, to look the other way, to defer to others needs, so as an adult I chose someone who knew how to take advantage of that.*

. . . .

*I knew my wife would never be happy just to be with one man. She made that obvious. But I loved her and she appeared to love me, so I just thought somehow I would handle it or she would grow out of this. As a kid I was willing to wait, to be patient for the moments when my father would give me attention. I was willing to take crumbs and maybe that is what I am doing today too.*

. . . .

*My dad had a lot of affairs, but his drug addiction was the main thing I was aware of. Now I have been married three times and all of my partners had multiple affairs, one was clearly a sex addict and two of the three were addicted to alcohol and/or other drugs.*

. . . .

*It was all about image growing up. Keep up the image. Don't have any dirty laundry anyone can see. Everything is nice. Everything is fine. So that is how I have functioned in my marriage, ignoring the reality of what was happening so I could just stay nice, clean, and fine.*

From the list below, write down five words you'd use to describe how you experienced the relationship you had with your mother when you were growing up. Using a different color pencil/pen, write down five words that describe how you experienced the relationship with your father when you were growing up. Now using a third color pencil/pen, write down the words that describe how you experience(d) your current/most current partner.

| | | |
|---|---|---|
| Respectful | Fun | Loving Caring |
| Committed | Angry | Fearful Fearful |
| Sad | Connected | Disconnected |
| Abusive/Hurtful | Rigid | Other |

- From words you chose that describe your relationship, do you notice any parallels in your relationships with a parent and with your significant other/spouse(s)? Describe.

If you grew up with blatant dysfunction such as that caused by addiction or abuse and find yourself in a similar situation or relationship as an adult, you may be particularly surprised and confused, as you so wanted to do it differently and possibly even told yourself that you had done so. What is most clear is that willpower alone is not enough to prevent repetition. It is possible that your relationship(s) is with someone who has the same addiction you were raised with, but because you were so young when your parent(s) was in the early stages of addiction you have no distinct recall of it. Therefore, in the relationship with your partner, you do not see the similarity to the relationship with your parent. Or, you are so focused on making sure you don't end up with someone like your mother or father who may have been addicted to alcohol and/or other drugs, that you are ever vigilant against choosing a person who appears to drink responsibly or doesn't drink or use drugs at all, ignoring the signs of other addictive behaviors.

Perhaps you were aware of the behavior and recognize the similarity to what you experienced in your childhood, but have impoverished expectations due to low self-esteem, wherein you don't expect more from a partner. You see yourself as a survivor; you believe you can tolerate and handle things. Your tolerance may be so high that it leads you to overlook and minimize neglectful and rejecting behavior through excuses you make that let the addict off the hook.

**EXAMPLES**

*I am tough; I just look beyond the times he is violent and tell myself he doesn't really want to be this way. As a consequence, I have raised two children in an abusive home and today one is an addict and the other may be on his way to addiction.*

. . . .

*I made sure I didn't marry an alcoholic. Instead, I married the guy who seemed to have it all together. He was good looking, the class president, who became a CEO of a company, and still looks good to others. He doesn't abuse alcohol or take other drugs, but he has been having sex with prostitutes throughout our entire marriage.*

- What is your story? Beginning with your mid-adolescent age years, name the people with whom you had significant relationships and to what degree each was part of a repeating pattern.

- The following are traits common to partners who experienced abandonment as a child and then again in relationships. Write down the trait you identify with in your current relationship, and note if this trait was learned prior to this relationship.

## Traits

Overlook (deny, rationalize, minimize) behavior that hurts deeply.

Appear cheerful when hurting.

Make excuses for (the) hurtful behavior.

Avoid conflict to minimize anger.

Tolerate inappropriate and hurtful behavior (especially over time).

Prioritize the needs of others over self.

Take care of others.

Discount own perceptions by giving others the benefit of the doubt.

Believe you have no options available.

Believe you are at fault, therefore it is your job to find the answers.

Not ask for help or difficulty asking for help.

Accommodate.

• What other traits do you think you learned prior to this relationship?

As you do the work in this book, you will develop more self-esteem and know yourself in a way you have not been able to previously. You have started a different journey now and by owning your history you are leaving behind the old script.

## Family Tree

*Here is a tool that reinforces and offers greater clarity about how the roots of codependency and addictive behaviors span generations, preceding present-day relationships. It is valuable in learning more about your family and also understanding the strength of dysfunction as it moves through generations. By doing your part in recovery you are a part of changing this family scenario.*

A family is like a large house with many rooms. The family you have now, as an adult, is the central living area; in fact, the "family room." Each of the other rooms of the house represents the previous and new generations of your family, all of which connect directly or indirectly. Through the doors to those rooms pass family traditions, secrets, and stories about what is and isn't true, and what a person should and shouldn't do. In your recovery there will be many insights not just about your present relationship, but about yourself and your family.

The language used today is certainly not the language used in past generations. Yesterday's womanizer is today's sex addict; yesterday's partier is today's alcoholic; yesterday's neurotic is today's person with anxiety disorder or codependent. Depending on the social and emotional connections within the generations, information may or may not have been forthcoming and the dynamics of stigma and shame often prevent history from being passed down accurately. Yet today, when asked, most people can look back and identify patterns about their family lineage.

To look at the possibility of how family issues can pass through the generations, it is helpful to do a family tree known as a genogram. As you do this exercise you may find yourself feeling disloyal. Whether as a child or an adult, when it comes to discussing family, loyalty often comes into play. By committing to paper your perceptions or information you have gathered, you are not saying family members are bad or wrong, you are simply acknowledging the maladies that pervade family systems. In some cases, what has occurred has certainly been hurtful, but that does not take away from the strengths inherent in any family system.

Create a Family Tree (see example below), and to the best of your ability fill it in with the names of those you can identify, and acknowledge those whose names you don't know as "unknown name." Add as many lines as you need.

## FAMILY TREE

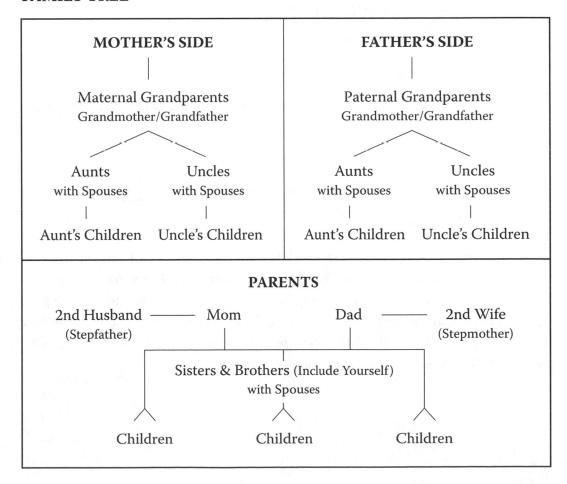

After you complete the Family Tree, use the abbreviations listed below and place the initials of the specific addiction or traumas next to the names of family members who you have reason to suspect or know experienced them.

SA = Substance addictions (alcohol or other drugs)

ED = Eating disorder/compulsive overeating, anorexia, or bulimia

SXA = Sex addiction

GA = Gambling addiction

WA = Work addiction

CO = Codependent, partner of addicted person (other than sex)

COSA = Partner of sex addict

SAS = Sex abuse survivor

SO = Sexual offender/child molester or rapist

RR = Rigid religious beliefs

PD = Premature death (premature death means prior to what would be the norm). Note the cause of death as well.

IN = In recovery from any of the above

CI = Chronic illness or disability, either physical or mental (or both)


In doing a Family Tree you often face a lack of information. Family secrets are common, be they due to taboos within the family system about sharing information or shame related to the behavior. As you realize there is missing information or have new questions or insights, it can lead you to seek more knowledge about your family. It also allows you to be more accepting, without judgment, about the difficulties that exist in the present-day generation. By admitting the reality of what is, you deflate the power of secrecy.

What did you learn about your family? Did it lead to any new insights?

## Knowing Your Emotional Self

*We will now help you take a look at the influences you have had that affect your ability to identify, tolerate, and express various feelings. You will look at the predominant feelings of sadness, anger, fear, guilt, and loneliness. This exercise also allows you to look at the repetition that may be occurring with a partner.*

The ability to tolerate, identify, and then express feelings appropriately is about honoring your emotional self. Your ability to be comfortable with your emotional self and have the skills to identify and appropriately express feelings is strongly influenced by early childhood experiences. This exercise gives you an opportunity to recognize the role of generational repetition in this area, as well as lead to greater self-awareness and direction for your recovery practice.

### SADNESS

Create three columns in your journal (see example below) and note the degree for feeling sadness as you experienced it as a child in your family and as an adult today.

**EXAMPLE**

| Childhood | SADNESS | Adult |
|---|---|---|
| | Very Sad | |
| | Sad | |
| | Somewhat Sad | |
| | Rarely Sad | |
| | Never Sad | |

- Write down those behaviors that describe what you did as a child when you felt sad.

- Write down those behaviors that describe what you do today when you feel sad.

EXAMPLES

| Behaviors I performed as a child when I felt sad. | Behaviors I perform today when I feel sad. |
|---|---|
| • Cried when I was alone. | • Cry when I'm alone. |
| • Cried in front of others. | • Cry in front of others. |
| • Went to bed. | • Go to bed. |
| • Took a walk. | • Take a walk. |
| • Told someone about my sadness. | • Tell someone about my sadness. |
| • Other. | • Other. |

- Describe how your parent(s) responded to you when you felt sad as a child.

EXAMPLES

| When I felt sad my mom usually | When I felt sad my dad usually |
|---|---|
| • Never noticed. | • Never noticed. |
| • Noticed, but ignored it. | • Noticed, but ignored it. |
| • Made me feel embarrassed or ashamed. | • Made me feel embarrassed or ashamed. |
| • Made me feel better. | • Made me feel better. |
| • Other. | • Other. |

• Describe how your partner (most recent) responds to you when you feel sad.

EXAMPLE

**When I feel sad, my partner usually**

• Never notices.

• Notices, but ignores it.

• Makes me feel embarrassed or ashamed.

• Makes me feel better.

• Other.

• In your response to sadness, do you notice childhood patterns being repeated in adult life? Describe.

## ANGER

Create three columns in your journal (see example below) and note the degree for feeling anger as you experienced it as a child in your family and as an adult today.

EXAMPLE

| Childhood | **ANGER** | Adult |
|---|---|---|
| | Very Angry | |
| | Angry | |
| | Somewhat Angry | |
| | Rarely Angry | |
| | Never Angry | |

• Write down those behaviors that describe what you did as a child when you felt anger.

- Write down those behaviors that describe what you do today when you feel anger.

EXAMPLES

| Behaviors I performed as a child when I felt anger. | Behaviors I perform today when I feel anger. |
|---|---|
| • Pouted. | • Pout. |
| • Screamed (at whom?). | • Scream (at whom?). |
| • Was sarcastic. | • Am sarcastic. |
| • Told the person with whom I was angry directly about my anger. | • Tell the person with whom I am angry directly about my anger. |
| • Hit harder on the ball field (or other sport). | • Push my self harder at work or sports. |
| • Ate to stuff my anger. | • Eat to stuff my anger. |
| • Ran away. | • Run away. |
| • Other. | • Other. |

- Describe how your parent(s) responded to you when you felt anger as a child.

EXAMPLES

| When I felt angry my mom usually | When I felt angry my dad usually |
|---|---|
| • Never noticed. | • Never noticed. |
| • Noticed, but ignored it. | • Noticed, but ignored it. |
| • Made me feel embarrassed or ashamed. | • Made me feel embarrassed or ashamed. |
| • Made me feel better. | • Made me feel better. |
| • Other. | • Other. |

- Describe how your partner (most recent) responds to you when you feel anger.

EXAMPLES

**When I feel angry, my partner usually**

- Never notices.

- Notices, but ignores it.

- Makes me feel embarrassed or ashamed.

- Makes me feel better.

- Other.

- In your response to anger, do you notice childhood patterns being repeated in adult life? Describe.

**FEAR**

Create three columns in your journal (see example below) and note the degree for feeling fear as you experienced it as a child in your family and as an adult today.

EXAMPLE

| Childhood | FEAR | Adult |
|---|---|---|
| | Very Fearful | |
| | Fearful | |
| | Somewhat Fearful | |
| | Rarely Fearful | |
| | Never Fearful | |

- Write down those behaviors that describe what you did as a child when you felt fear.

• Write down those behaviors that describe what you do today when you feel fear.

EXAMPLES

| Behaviors I performed as a child when I felt afraid. | Behaviors I perform today when I feel afraid. |
|---|---|
| • Acted like I was not afraid. | • Act like I'm not afraid. |
| • Cried. | • Cry. |
| • Got angry. | • Get angry. |
| • Hid. (Where?) | • Hide. (Where?) |
| • Told someone about my fear. | • Tell someone about my fear. |
| • Other. | • Other. |

• Describe how your parent(s) responded to you when you felt fear as a child.

EXAMPLES

| When I felt afraid my mom usually | When I felt afraid my dad usually |
|---|---|
| • Never noticed. | • Never noticed. |
| • Noticed, but ignored it. | • Noticed, but ignored it. |
| • Made me feel embarrassed or ashamed. | • Made me feel embarrassed or ashamed. |
| • Made me feel better. | • Made me feel better. |
| • Other. | • Other. |

• Describe how your partner (most recent) responds to you when you are afraid.

**EXAMPLES**

**When I am fearful, my partner usually**

_____

• Never notices.

• Notices, but ignores it.

• Makes me feel embarrassed or ashamed.

• Makes me feel better.

• Other.

• In your response to fear, do you notice childhood patterns being repeated in adult life? Describe.

# GUILT

Create three columns in your journal (see example below) and note the degree for feeling guilt as you experienced it as a child in your family and as an adult today.

**EXAMPLE**

| Childhood | **GUILT** | Adult |
|---|---|---|
| | Very Guilty | |
| | Guilty | |
| | Somewhat Guilty | |
| | Rarely Guilty | |
| | Never Guilty | |

• Write down those behaviors that describe what you did as a child when you felt guilt.

• Write down those behaviors that describe what you do today when you feel guilt.

EXAMPLES

| Behaviors I performed as a child when I felt guilty. | Behaviors I perform today when I feel guilty. |
| --- | --- |
| • Ate to stuff my feelings of guilt. | • Eat to stuff my feelings of guilt. |
| • Hid. (Where?) | • Hide. (Where?) |
| • Apologized. | • Apologize. |
| • Cleaned my room. | • Clean the house. |
| • Tried to act "real good." | • Try to act "real good." |
| • Other. | • Other. |

• Describe how your parent(s) responded to you when you felt guilty as a child.

EXAMPLES

| When I felt guilty my mom usually | When I felt guilty my dad usually |
| --- | --- |
| • Never knew. | • Never knew. |
| • Reinforced my guilt by blaming me for things I did not do. | • Reinforced my guilt by blaming me for things I did not do. |
| • Made me feel even more guilt. | • Made me feel even more guilt. |
| • Punished me even if I was not at fault. | • Punished me even if I was not at fault. |
| • Made me feel that I was not responsible, therefore, helping to lessen my guilt. | • Made me feel that I was not responsible, therefore, helping to lessen my guilt. |
| • Other. | • Other. |

• Describe how your partner (most recent) responds to you when you feel guilt.

EXAMPLES

**When I feel guilty, my partner usually**

• Never knows.

• Reinforces my guilt by blaming me for things I did not do.

• Makes me feel even more guilt.

• Blames me even if I was not at fault.

• Makes me feel that I was not responsible, therefore, helping to lessen my guilt.

• Other.

• In your response to guilt, do you notice childhood patterns being repeated in adult life? Describe.

## LONELINESS

Create three columns in your journal (see example below) and note the degree for feeling lonely as you experienced it as a child in your family and as an adult today.

EXAMPLE

| Childhood | **LONELINESS** | Adult |
|---|---|---|
| | Very Lonely | |
| | Lonely | |
| | Somewhat Lonely | |
| | Rarely Lonely | |
| | Never Lonely | |

• Write down those behaviors that describe what you did as a child when you felt lonely.

- Write down those behaviors that describe what you do today when you feel lonely.

EXAMPLES

| Behaviors I performed as a child when I felt lonely. | Behaviors I perform today when I feel lonely. |
| --- | --- |
| • Cried. | • Act out, e.g., have affairs, go on spending sprees, etc. |
| • Took a walk. | • Self-medicate, e.g., eat food, use alcohol and/or other drugs, etc. |
| • Spent time with my pet. | • Isolate. |
| • Isolated myself. | • Stay busy. |
| • Reached out to someone. | • Reach out to someone. |
| • Other. | • Other. |

- Describe how your parent(s) responded to you when you felt lonely as a child.

EXAMPLES

| When I felt lonely my mom usually | When I felt lonely my dad usually |
| --- | --- |
| • Never knew. | • Never knew. |
| • Knew but did nothing. | • Knew but did nothing. |
| • Said I had no reason to feel lonely. | • Said I had no reason to feel lonely. |
| • Made me feel worse. | • Made me feel worse. |
| • Made me feel better. | • Made me feel better. |
| • Other. | • Other. |

- Describe how your partner (most recent) responds to you when you are lonely.

**EXAMPLES**

**When I am lonely, my partner usually**

- Never knows.

- Knows but does nothing.

- Spends time with me.

- Makes me feel better.

- Makes me feel worse.

- Other.

- In your response to loneliness, do you notice childhood patterns being repeated in adult life? Describe.

Doing this exercise gives you the opportunity to recognize how emotional patterns repeat themselves. It may demonstrate that you abandon yourself as you were once abandoned and you pick a partner who abandons you in similar ways. You may also recognize, regardless of abandonment, that you have found some healthy ways to cope with your feelings. It is important in this healing process to acknowledge that you don't need to continue to repeat any forms of abandonment; you deserve to live your life differently today. Feelings are here to be indicators of what you need, and you want to listen to them. You want to be free to acknowledge them.

## Honoring Your Needs

*In order to get your needs met, it will be necessary to develop your ability to identify and attach value to those needs. In this section, you will explore messages you internalized about beliefs and the degree to which your basic childhood needs were met. You will look at how this has influenced your ability to identify and honor your needs today.*

In our humanity all people have needs, the most basic ones being food, clothing, and shelter. Needs permeate all areas of life; recognizing and getting them met via others and attending to needs gives you the opportunity to thrive, allowing you to embrace and enjoy the opportunities life offers.

To meet your own needs it's important to be able to define what they are. You have needs relationally, emotionally, mentally, physically, and spiritually. To have a healthy relationship you *need* to be heard, to have respect, and to have the freedom in which to own your voice. For self-care, you *need* to have time for yourself and time with dear friends. To be emotionally healthy, you *need* to know what constitutes healthy boundaries and be able to tolerate your feeling states. Mentally, you *need* stimulation. Learning new things or expanding upon already developed ideas challenges you to grow. Spiritually, you *need* time for spiritual practice. It may be that over time you have found those needs have gradually eroded and have been replaced by other immediate needs such as trying to save your relationship or being consumed with parenting.

Getting your needs met is only possible when you have the ability to identify those needs and attach value to them. Through a variety of experiences both in childhood and adult life, you often learn to dismiss your own needs and become increasingly more occupied with attempting to meet the needs of others.

From the statements below, write down those that most fit you and provide examples of how this is so.

- My needs are important.
- If I don't attach value to my needs they won't get met.
- Other people's needs are more important than mine.
- I'm always more focused on other people's needs, it seems they are always in such a crisis and someone has to make it better.
- I don't know what it means to have needs.
- Am not sure what I "really" need.

The capacity to identify and own your needs, as well as the ability to attach value to them, is optimally achieved in a household that functions to meet the needs of its individuals.

A healthy functioning family system consists of primary caregivers who are consistently attentive to a child's needs growing up. That does not mean a child is given everything he or she asks for, but rather that because the child's parents understand developmentally what is in the best interest of the child's emotional, social, and spiritual growth, they strive to protect and care for the child throughout his or her growing-up years.

What messages did you receive about having needs? How has that been hurtful or helpful to you in your present-day relationship?

**EXAMPLES**
*Children are meant to be seen and not heard.*

•  •  •  •

*It's not okay to complain or cry.*

•  •  •  •

*I'm on my own. Mom is too busy to care about me.*

• The following is a list of emotional, social, intellectual, and physical needs all children have. As a child, to what degree were those needs met? In your journal, write the number next to the needs below. (One (1) being the least and five (5) being the most.)

- • Sense of safety/security
- • Affirmation (told what was liked about you and/or your behavior)
- • Opportunity to play
- • Able to laugh
- • Encouraged to question
- • Encouraged to make age-appropriate decisions
- • Able to stand up for myself
- • Able to express my feelings
- • Believed my feelings would be heard
- • Knew I could ask for help
- • Had time for myself

- Have my own boundaries/able to set my own limits
- Believed I was special to others
- Experienced appropriate touch
- Encouraged and supported to learn
- Other (name them)

- For any needs you rated three (3) or less, how has this affected you in your adult life?

- Write what you need today in the different areas of your life?

  Physically I need

  Emotionally I need

  Intellectually I need

  Relationally I need

  Spiritually I need

- Recognizing that you have specific needs today, how do you see yourself attending to them?

Stating what you need is the first step to those needs being met. Attaching value to them is the next step. You are on your way.

## Trusting Your Own Perceptions

*Much of the distrust of your own perceptions probably began long before your current relationship. If that is accurate, it is more ingrained and more difficult to recognize in yourself. Here you will begin the process of recognizing the degree to which it has been a life-long defense and now a well-honed skill. This insight can reinforce a greater willingness to trust yourself more rather than giving others the benefit of the doubt that has so often led to your victimization.*

When you have lived with sexual betrayal, unknown to you, you were caught in a world of secrets. Initially, you may have questioned or suspected something, but were told you were wrong, lied to further, or made to feel feelings that weren't true for you. Discounting your perceptions and giving others the benefit of the doubt comes more easily for many partners as it is often a dynamic learned in childhood. In this exercise you will explore some of the early ways in which you learned to doubt yourself and readily accept the perceptions or reality imposed upon you by others.

Children are innately dependent on their caregivers. The caregiver's position is of great influence and with it comes the responsibility to do no harm to the child. From here, children develop trust and feel safe about their environment and are better prepared over time to meet the challenges of the world. But if the caregiver is unable to provide a consistently safe and nurturing environment for the child to develop, the child's perceptions are based on the lack of safety he or she experiences in the world. Out of that environment the child's reality-testing is compromised and he or she gives others the benefit of the doubt rather than trusting him- or herself.

### EXAMPLES

*You see your mother crying and ask her why she is sad, and she tells you she isn't sad, she just has something in her eyes.*

. . . .

*You tell your parents you are scared after listening to them arguing loudly, and they tell you that you have no reason to be scared.*

. . . .

*You are sad and crying and your parents tell you that you have nothing to cry about, and in fact, if you keep it up they will really give you something to cry about. In this case, not only are your feelings invalidated, but you are threatened if you maintain this emotional state.*

. . . .

*When your father is unusually absent, you are told he is on a work trip when in fact your mother doesn't know where he is.*

Another way children are told their perceptions don't matter is through verbal abuse. If they are told they are stupid and that others are smarter than they are, or if they experienced a lot of criticism or ridicule, then they learn to *not* trust who they are but who others think they are.

This treatment leads to self-doubt, insecurity, and low self-esteem. When you don't believe you have the right to your own thoughts you become vulnerable to someone else's. This might feel normal because it is familiar to you. If so, this leads to problems in self-perception, reality-testing, and boundary confusion with others.

Of course parents get impatient and at times lack the skills to appropriately handle situations. But we are not talking about occasional events or circumstances. We are talking about a pattern of behavior exhibited by the parent over time. The child comes to anticipate these types of responses from the parent and develops maladaptive coping skills accordingly. "Mom gets mad when I ask to play with my friends, so I'll stop asking." This treatment results in the child believing his or her needs are not important and his or her reality is not his or her own, but that of the caregiver. Trusting your own perceptions is a learned behavior, and if you were made to feel wrong and discouraged from trusting your voice, then your reality becomes skewed and based on how others see it rather than how you experience it.

Give examples of when your perceptions were invalidated or greatly altered during your childhood.

Looking over the examples you identified, ask yourself how the messages contributed to certain inflexible beliefs you carry with you and how they affect your relationships. For example, if you are told your father is on a work trip when in fact your mother doesn't know where he is, or told that a car wreck was caused by an animal jumping out into the road when you overheard a conversation that says otherwise, those distorted truths could lead to "I need to trust the authority person over myself." And you may perceive your partner as the person of greater authority, leaving you to chronically defer to him or her.

When you are told you have nothing to be afraid about at a time that is very frightening, that distorted truth may lead to a belief that says, "I have nothing to be afraid of when I have something to be afraid of." You may have learned to dismiss your feelings so readily that today it has fueled an inability to even recognize feelings in or about your relationship.

If you come to distrust the way you view things, you will in general dismiss your intuition and not feel confident to speak to what you think and feel.

Give examples of dismissing your intuition that have occurred in your most current relationship. How did that make you feel and what did you think? What was the outcome of that for you?

- Identify times in which you stayed true to yourself and didn't let others tell you how to think or feel or act in a given situation. These were times you held on to your perception and didn't allow someone else to take it away from you. How did that make you feel and what did you think? What was the outcome of that for you?

Learning to trust your own perceptions and giving yourself the benefit of the doubt is paramount to your recovery. As one partner said, *"It isn't so important I trust him as it is I learn to trust me."* Obviously she wants to trust her spouse, but she is right. She goes on to say, *"Today in my recovery if I have a feeling, an intuition, or something doesn't feel right, I make sure I speak up. Before, I would just remain silent. Now, it is not okay not to be heard. I have learned my voice matters."*

## Recognizing Unhealthy Boundaries

*It is often easier to recognize a lack of healthy boundaries when you recognize boundary distortions and violations that were prevalent in your growing-up years. As you work through this section, you will further your understanding of boundaries and learn how to set healthy boundaries today.*

The need for nonnegotiable boundaries was addressed in Chapter One. But boundaries are a subject that goes beyond the rigid ones you needed initially to feel more stable. In order to get your needs met in general, you need to have healthy boundaries and have the ability to set limits. Partners of those struggling with sex addiction often have few boundaries, or highly distorted ones. Typically this preceded your current relationship and often began in childhood. When you have been raised with a lack of healthy boundaries, and as a result have no modeling for what is healthy, it is normal to tolerate hurtful behavior and not even recognize boundary distortion.

Healthy boundaries are experienced on a continuum. This can range from having a lack of boundaries leading to enmeshment, to being walled off with unhealthy boundaries, experiencing disconnection. When there is no distinction between you and another person, and you are expected to think, feel, and be as they are, that is enmeshment. When your mother is angry, you are supposed to be angry. When your mother wants tomato soup for dinner, you are supposed to want tomato soup. When your mother chooses green as her favorite color, you are supposed to like green as your favorite color. When there is no child-to-adult distinction, and as a child you were a parent's peer, then that is enmeshment. When your mother tells you it is your job to get in the car and go find your father, who did not come home, that is enmeshment; you are used to taking care of her and fighting her battles. When you are expected to be there for your mother in her pain and she does not find support with other adults, then that's enmeshment. When your father rejects your dreams and demands you follow in the path of his unfulfilled dream, that's enmeshment.

On the flip side, people in your family may have had little desire for connection for a variety of reasons so that they didn't bond and are emotionally disconnected. You didn't even know when your father had a major disappointment at work; you didn't know how your mother felt when her mother died. When your parents broke up, your father just disappeared and there weren't even good-byes. They didn't respond to your accomplishments at school; you were met with silence. They didn't offer any nurturance, curiosity, or support at times in which you were noticeably sad or angry. That is emotional disconnection.

- While you were growing up, would you describe your relationship with your mother to be one of healthy boundaries, enmeshment, or disconnection? Explain.

- While you were growing up, would you describe your relationship with your father to be one of healthy boundaries, enmeshment, or disconnection? Explain.

Unhealthy boundaries create confusion about who is responsible for what, adding to distortion of guilt and shame. As a result of living with chronic boundary violation/distortion, one is often unskilled in setting boundaries or is disrespectful and intrusive of others' boundaries. People raised with unhealthy boundaries often normalize hurtful behavior and don't recognize boundary distortion. It is easy for them to lack protective boundaries, setting them up for victimization—or because of a lack of containment boundaries, they become hurtful toward others.

The following are examples of unhealthy boundaries on the part of others toward you. Write down whether or not you were subjected to and/or experienced any of these unhealthy boundaries as a child and in your most current relationship.

**Emotional**

Feelings denied.

Told what you can and cannot feel.

Raged at.

Criticized.

Belittled.

Lack of expectations.

Terrorized.

Other.

**Spiritual**

Went against personal values/rights to please others.

Taught to believe in a punishing higher power.

No spiritual guidance.

No sense of gratitude.

Not taught to pray or meditate.

Dogmatic/rigid doctrine.

Other.

**Sexual**

Lacked sexual information during puberty.

Given misinformation about your body and your development.

Shamed for being wrong gender.

Exposed to pornography.

Subjected to sexualized comments.

Subjected to sexual abuse.

Witnessed abuse of others.

Other.

## Physical

Received touch you did not want.

Not taught appropriate hygiene.

Experienced abuse, such as pushing, hitting, kicking, pinching, slapping, etc.

Excessive tickling.

Deprived of touch.

Witnessed abuse of others.

Other.

## Intellectual

Denied information.

Not allowed to make mistakes.

Not encouraged to question.

Called names or compared to others.

Encouraged to follow a parent's dream rather than your own.

Other.

Reflecting now on your adult relationships, look at the examples below and write down if and how you experience others violating your boundaries.

## Emotional

Feelings denied, disrespected, or unacknowledged.

Told what you can and cannot feel.

Raged at.

Criticized.

Belittled.

Terrorized.

Other.

## Spiritual

Coerced to go against personal values or rights to please another.

Your spiritual journey not supported and possibly sabotaged.

Not offered shared opportunity to develop sense of belonging/being part of a greater whole.

Manipulation of religious principles.

Feel as if there is a hole in your soul.

Other.

## Sexual

Shamed, criticized for your sexual performance.

Exposed to sexual behavior you didn't want to engage in.

Recipient of controlling sex, withholding, angry sex.

Denied sexual expression.

Unknown exposure to sexually transmitted diseases.

Other.

## Physical

Received touch you did not want.

Experienced abuse, pushing, hitting, kicking, pinching, slapping.

Excessive tickling.

Deprived of touch.

Other.

## Intellectual

Denied information.

Not allowed to make mistakes.

Not encouraged to question.

Called names.

Other.

## Relationship

Falling in love with anyone who shows interest.

Allowing someone to take as much as they can from you.

Letting others define your reality.

Believing others can anticipate your needs.

Being subjected to walls of silent treatment, anger, barrage of words, etc.

Other.

While no one wants to see themselves as being offensive toward others, it is very possible you have not been respectful of and/or crossed other's boundaries. Take a look at the list below, and write down any of the boundary violations that demonstrate a lack of containment and intrusive boundaries that you have engaged in your relationships.

## Emotional

Deny the feelings of others.

Tell others what they can and cannot feel.

Verbally rage.

Criticize.

Belittle.

Don't expect from others.

Other.

## Spiritual

Ask another to go against personal values or rights to please you.

Dismiss other's spiritual journey as unimportant.

Manipulate with religious precepts.

Other.

## Sexual

Shame others for their sexual performance.

Use sex to punish or garner control.

Sexually objectify others.

Sexually abusive.

Other.

## Physical

Abuse another, e.g., push, hit, kick, pinch, slap.

Deprive intimate partner of healthy touch.

Invade privacy.

Other.

## Intellectual

Withhold information.

No tolerance for mistakes.

Not allow others to question.

Name calling, compare them to others.

Expect another to follow your dream rather than his or her own.

Other.

## Relationship

Avoid healthy communication through walls of silence, anger, barrage of words.

Define others' realities for them.

Not listen with respect.

Other.

You have had a lot to think about as you completed this exercise. What has impacted you the most? Look at the statements on the following page and write the one that most identifies you.

- I mostly lack boundaries to protect myself.

- I have difficulty respecting the boundaries of others.

- I have difficulty with both protecting myself and respecting others' boundaries.

- Knowing your vulnerabilities around boundaries, what are your top three priorities in addressing them? Keep these top three priorities in mind. You will have the opportunity to explore developing healthy boundaries further in the next section.

Your recovery often includes learning things for the first time. Developing healthier boundaries takes time and practice.

## Willingness to Explore More

*We will now ask you to identify what you would like to continue to address as it relates to family of origin issues. We encourage you to go beyond what you can do in this book, knowing that addressing these issues will ultimately provide the foundation for your recovery. There are many books and different forms of therapy that will be helpful in the process.*

How you react to your current situation is strongly influenced by unconscious childhood experiences and internalized beliefs. Therefore it is important to be able to voice childhood experiences and grieve the pain associated as a part of separating the past from influencing what is happening in the present. What you do, think, or feel in the present is readily tainted by unfinished business with others. You want to be able to deal with current situations without being influenced by your past.

You are not dismissing your partner's behavior by taking the time to address this part of your life. You owe it to yourself, this relationship, and any other relationship to do what you can to put the past behind you.

While you cannot do in-depth trauma work in a book, identifying whether or not you think this is an important issue for you and beginning to identify the focus of the trauma work is a place to begin.

- Are there specific issues such as abuse, abandonment, boundaries, feelings, etc. you want to read more about or address further in therapy? If you answered yes to this question, then name those items you want to read more about or address further in therapy.

- Name the specific persons and issues with which you have unfinished family of origin issues. This does not mean you meet with them directly, but would certainly mean you need to look at what your feelings and possible subsequent behaviors are that are related to this lack of resolution.

If you are considering therapy there are many different types you can explore to address unfinished family of origin issues. Today clinical and research experience tells us that nontraditional talking therapies are an integral and effective long-term approach to addressing abandonment and abuse histories. There are many such modalities. They range from art therapy to movement and dance therapies. It may be a therapy that includes more journaling, writing exercises, or use of visual imagery. Many therapists find the use of eye movement desensitization and reprocessing (EMDR), somatic experiencing (SE), and energy psychology (EFT, TFT, etc.) to be important adjunctive components. The Resources section on page 233 contains a list that can help direct you toward such therapies, as well as recommended readings.

Attending to family of origin issues is a big and an important step that most partners will ultimately choose to address. You don't have to do it right now, but we encourage you to be open to it as a part of your ongoing recovery process. You have begun the process just by completing this section of the book. You deserve to feel good about yourself for your openness and willingness to seek recovery. It is painful to address material that is emotionally laden, material that calls to mind an even more vulnerable age and stage of development. You are to be commended.

# CHAPTER FIVE

# Taking Charge of Your Life

You have been building a foundation of greater strength that will serve you well in taking charge of your own life, but as you meet the challenges of daily life, you still need to tackle tough decisions and significant aspects of healing related to the relationship. This section offers you a framework for much of what you have wondered about and questioned. It will help diminish confusion about important pieces of your recovery. It will aid you in identifying whether or not you need more disclosure; help you to identify boundaries that strengthen your recovery; and help you be less frightened of the question you are going to ask yourself: do I stay or leave?

Because of the deception and the many defenses that have evolved over time in your relationship, our goal is to help you develop a picture of what creates healthy intimacy and sexuality. Knowing your roadblocks to intimacy will help you to move through them. Further in this chapter we help you address your concern for children. For any parent, one of the "biggies" is the concern for the kids—either regarding the impact on them or what to say to them. While so many of these topics are emotionally laden, acknowledging the concern and having some direction will make this a less painful and confusing time.

## Disclosure: Knowing the Scope of the Addiction

*Structured disclosure is defined as a psychologically safe way to hear from the sex addict the extent of the behavior. By this time, it is likely that you have experienced some form of disclosure, possibly mediated professionally, but often out of despair and duress. You have the opportunity here to consider whether or not a mediated and structured disclosure is something that would be helpful to you. These exercises will help you to better understand the value of disclosure and how best to engage in a healthy disclosure process.*

There came a critical moment when you could no longer deny that you have been repeatedly betrayed over a period of time. This pivotal moment was most likely preceded by an event(s) where you discovered or were told information previously kept from you. You were unprepared for what you were to learn. As the secrets unraveled before you, intense feelings, unending questions, and intrusive thoughts engulfed you, leaving you at a loss as to what to do next. You questioned whether you knew all there was to know and whether the extent and scope of the addictive behaviors had been disclosed.

Regardless of how you found out about the lies, either through discovery or disclosure, most likely you were emotionally unprepared. If you were told additional information at different times, it created a staggered effect, each time revictimizing you. When unplanned disclosures occur, it often occurs at times of extreme stress for both you and the addict. The aftermath often leads to more unanswered questions, assumptions, and fears that if left unaddressed can create further unnecessary harm.

## STRUCTURED DISCLOSURE

As the field of sexual addiction treatment has grown, so too has the awareness and recognition of the needs of partners. No place is this better understood than in the realm of disclosure—the manner in how you are given the information about what has occurred. Example after example has revealed that when information is shared without safety guidelines built into the process, the aftermath results in unnecessary damage. Clinicians are recognizing more than ever the rationale for and importance of a structured disclosure (SD), a psychologically safe way to hear from the sex addict regarding the extent of his or her behavior. Additionally, partners are becoming better advocates for what they need, and have played an instrumental role in voicing these concerns as a means of recovering from deception.

You have a right to know what it is you are facing, as well as the extent of the behaviors. To make an informed decision for yourself and your relationship it is imperative that you have the facts, and gather them in a way that is helpful to you. The purpose and primary goal of a SD is for you to have your questions answered and to provide a timeline of the addict's history pertaining to his or her sexual addiction. It is intended to answer questions about the *nature*, *scope*, and *extent* of the behavior *over time*. It is a planned and anticipated event involving the consent of both you and the addict. If one of you chooses not to do it, then it cannot go forward.

Although the primary goal of SD is for you, it has other benefits as well. It is an integral step in the addict's recovery in developing integrity through honesty. If the relationship is headed toward the likelihood of reconciliation, it can be a bridge in this process since for the first time both witness the addict's truthfulness as never before. The partner will often experience the addict taking responsibility for the first time, without excuses, denial, justification, and/or blame for his or her actions.

Ultimately, it is you who will know best whether disclosure is right and needed for your situation or not. The information and questions offered here will facilitate in that exploration process. Knowing how, when, where, and why helps in discerning what will best assist you in moving toward greater clarity and truth. It's the opposite of being unaware. Whether or not you decide to do an SD, you are already reversing the tide of deception's effect on your life by being involved and informed in the process.

The following are situations or circumstances where disclosure may *not* be warranted:

1. You feel you have enough information.

2. It's already been done.

3. You have decided to leave the relationship and to engage in disclosure feels like reliving the past.

4. You are already in the process of divorce.

5. You had a relationship in the past with a sex addict and are working through issues that remain unresolved today.

6. Your partner is unwilling to be involved.

If you identified with any of the above statements, describe what feelings emerged.

## STEPS IN PLANNING FOR STRUCTURED DISCLOSURE

SD is intended to be done with the guidance and direction of a trained professional who specializes in treating sex addiction. The clinician addresses the rationale and timing of it at the beginning of treatment. It is discussed as a goal to work toward, often within the first year of recovery. The timing of it is dependent on various factors; the most important is the addict's recovery. Addicts need to be fully engaged in their recovery and able to be as forthright as possible. This is often not doable when an addict is new to recovery, or if he or she slips or relapses. All of these are considerations that can postpone, stall, or circumvent the timing and/or rationale for SD.

One of the biggest concerns for the partner is the length of time from entering treatment until the time SD occurs. That waiting period can feel as if you are under the control of another, as though once again you are being kept in the dark. The timing and delay is to give you the best and most thorough history, with the emphasis on the facts that have occurred over time. It is also for both parties to be emotionally prepared.

Typically a structured disclosure is done with two therapists, the addict's and yours. An experienced therapist who has done disclosures will have a format and will prepare you accordingly for what questions need to be answered. This preparatory phase readies you for what to expect in terms of possibilities of behaviors not told to you by the addict, as well as considerations for what you may need afterward. You'll confront your fears as well as evaluate the motivation and intention for some of your queries to which you are seeking answers from the addict.

## CATEGORIES AND DETAILS

The greatest preparation is on the addict's part as he or she works on a timeline of the facts focusing on the categories of behavior, when they began, at what point they escalated, etc. Attention is also given to particular details or circumstances that involved you and, if applicable, your children, directly or indirectly. Categories of behavior include,

- Flirting.
- Masturbation.
- Voyeurism and/or staring too long at other people.
- Strip clubs.
- Affairs, sexual and/or emotional.
- Phone sex.
- Cybersex: viewing porn, chat rooms, online to offline activity.
- Demand for sex from you.
- DVDs, video streaming on phone, computer, TV.
- Prostitution.
- Child pornography.
- Money spent on the addiction.
- Same-sex acting out (when addict identified as heterosexual).
- Other.

It is also important to know the *extent* and *duration* of the addiction.

1. For how long?
2. With whom?
3. How many sexual/emotional partners outside of the relationship?
4. How did behaviors begin, escalate? What were certain points where it escalated and why?

## WHEN DETAILS ARE INDICATED

The details you'll want to know are when those that have this information have the potential to put you at various forms of risk. The details pertain to aspects of the behavior that involve you, your health, physical safety, finances, legal ramifications, people known to you and/or your family, or social milieu.

**EXAMPLES**

- *Flirting with neighbors, which ones, did it go further?*

- *Prostitution: being told the sexual acts he or she engaged in; whether a condom was used, sexually transmitted diseases.*

- *Relationships with people known to you or to another family member; who, how long?*

- *Emotional/sexual affair: personal details as to what was shared about intimacies in your relationship; e.g., "Did she know about our child's illness?" "Did you tell him about my cancer diagnosis?" "Were there unplanned pregnancies?" "Are there any children?"*

- *Legal ramifications of the behavior, e.g., lawsuits, criminal charges.*

- *Money spent on him or her; how much? What gifts did you buy, e.g., jewelry, lingerie, etc.?*

- *What do you know about what your children know?*

When is a detail contraindicated? When it will have no bearing on the scope of the actions and has no direct impact on you.

**EXAMPLES**

- *How many sexual positions?*

- *How many times did you visit X (unless it relates to personal situation)?*

- *Did you tell him or her that you loved him or her?*

- *How many times did you tell him or her?*

- *What did he or she look like, blond or brunette?*

- *Other.*

If you have been in pain and have serious questions about what was involved and have been unable to move ahead in your recovery with the addict, then it is time to get current about the past in order to move forward in the relationship. Explore whether there is value or need for this and consider what it will mean for you and the relationship.

- Do you believe a structured disclosure is something you need, and if so, why? What do you feel you would gain by having structured disclosure? What do you feel you may lose by having a structured disclosure?

- Sometimes the process of learning about the behaviors brings up fears about what you might learn. If you are afraid of any certain categories or situations he or she may have been involved in, please write them out.

- If your worst fears become realized, what will that mean to you? What happens if you learn information that was unexpected?

By exploring whether structured disclosure is right for you and your situation, it is essential that you keep in mind that the goal is to bring an end to the larger questions that remain unanswered—questions as to the extent, scope, and nature of the sexual behaviors. An SD will never make up for having been deceived. The damage has been done and to consider reconciliation, it is necessary to bring closure to the past—not to forget it, but to feel informed and to put to rest questions that used to consume you.

The reasons for a disclosure may make sense for your situation. As you consider, plan, and anticipate SD, most likely you will experience more pain and uncertainty. You will also generate greater clarity and validation of the fears you've carried for some time. Many partners see the pain as bearable and worth the risk, as greater honesty brings potential health to the relationship. Many addicts and partners alike see that disclosure is pivotal to changing the direction of the relationship.

SD evens the playing field of the relationship, as work on the relationship in the present becomes the focus. It also offers you information to be able to make better decisions for yourself. Yet you need to assess your own situation. If you believe structured disclosure is indicated for your relationship, do not, we repeat, do not attempt to facilitate it between you and your partner alone. Seek help to properly prepare for what is involved. You deserve the truth and nothing less. The key to having an SD be a helpful process is timing and preparedness on both your parts through the guidance and direction of trained therapists who lead the way.

# Finding Freedom with Healthy Boundaries

*In this section you will gain a greater understanding of the purpose of boundaries and this will reinforce how with healthy boundaries you can act instead of react to situations; you can maintain your own integrity. It allows you to begin to move from the disruption of addiction to identifying the areas that need strengthening for your recovery.*

Boundaries are defined by who you are. They are ubiquitous and are a part of all you do and all the people you encounter. They can be conscious and unconscious, purposeful and reflexive. They differ depending on the context in which they're applied. As you learned in Chapter One, sometimes boundaries are nonnegotiable if safety is at issue. In Chapter Four, you explored the origins of unhealthy boundaries and the impact this had on you. Here you will turn your attention toward fostering healthy boundaries and explore areas where further growth and attention is needed. As you have increased your self-awareness, your thinking has put you in touch with all your relationships and has you questioning whether boundaries need to change as you have been changing.

Healthy boundaries are shaped and reflected by your preferences, thoughts, emotions, beliefs, needs, sensations, and values. If your boundaries were ignored, dependent on others, or conversely you couldn't accept someone else's limits, then it may be challenging and confusing to reflect on your likes and dislikes. Don't let that deter you. Be patient. Recognize the changes you have already made. You have identified nonnegotiables and understand some of the beliefs that influenced how you got here. Taking the next step further underscores your developing self-awareness.

Healthy boundaries are about flexibility and freedom, as they reflect your self-worth and help you to separate others' feelings and opinions from your own. Having a good understanding of your boundaries means you can act instead of react to situations and distinguish where you end, and another begins.

### EXAMPLE

*When Jane learned her husband had had slips with pornography, she'd react by checking his email and phone to see if he was continuing to act out. As her recovery progressed, she realized her behavior was making her feel worse about herself, as her focus was on him and not on herself. She reassessed her boundaries and made changes in how she reacted by thinking before she acted and by journaling her thoughts and feelings. She also waited until she could address her fears and concerns from a clear and direct place and not one of reactivity and high emotion. This helped her clarify her goals for herself and the relationship, i.e., did she want to live with someone who continued to act out?*

## VALUES INFORM BOUNDARIES

Boundaries start with certain beliefs or facts. They are

- *Essential* to the self.

- Your *responsibility.*

- *Respectful* of others' limits.

- Not perfect. *Mistakes* are okay.

- *Necessary* when physical, emotional, or psychological safety is in question.

Identify which of these beliefs you have more difficulty asserting. What makes it hard for you to do so?

### EXAMPLES
*I never knew what boundaries were for me. I felt I just had to go along with what others told me.*

. . . .

*My wife tells me all the time not to read her recovery material. I always felt I had a right to this. I can see now that this is a violation of her boundaries, something others have told me as well.*

- Would you like to behave differently? If so, what would it look like?

### EXAMPLE
*I would talk to my wife about my suspicions rather than looking at her recovery material as though I have a right to it. I don't have a right to do so, and I want to change this behavior of mine. I realized I would rather take what I feel I deserve (know the truth by looking through her things) than ask for what I need by talking to her.*

When boundaries are mutually understood and respected, this leads to greater life satisfaction and well-being. Boundaries allow you to feel close without being engulfed and *separate from,* but in *relationship to* those around you. Personal safety and security is at its highest.

Being a partner of a sex addict means that much of what you trusted was faulty. Fears that you may be betrayed again make you hesitant to take risks. Addiction created chaos, and peace and stability seemed out of reach. Your boundaries now reflect the betrayal, and rebuilding trust will be a slow process. It starts with believing in the *possibility* of trust and observing your partner's actions in recovery.

Consider what your life would look like without trauma and chaos or the effects of past violations. In order to do so, reflect on some important ingredients that contribute to making people happy, satisfied, and fulfilled.

From the list below, write down those attributes you value. Feel free to add your own.

| | | |
|---|---|---|
| Honesty | Solitude | Empathy |
| Integrity | Accountability | Forgiveness |
| Commitment | Courage | Humility |
| Wisdom | Faith | Responsibility |
| Contentment | Joy | Pleasure |

• Write about what those attributes mean to you.

**EXAMPLE**
*Kindness: I think it is important to be kind to others since it contributes to the good in the world. I like the term "pay it forward," where you do a kindness for others.*

· · · ·

*Integrity: I think it is important that you live on the outside the way you are on the inside. If you believe in being good and trustworthy, then choices and actions in the rest of your life reflect that belief.*

The following categories of boundaries are central to healing from sex addiction and will help you in labeling the areas of importance to your recovery.

1. **Emotional** boundaries define the self, ideas, feelings, and values. You set them by choosing how you allow people to treat you. Often, prior to addiction, your feelings were hidden from you or conversely, you tolerated a partner who withheld his or hers.

2. **Spiritual** boundaries allow you to define the spiritual path for yourself. They reflect your deepest, innermost self and can be expressed through a faith-based practice or not.

3. **Sexual** boundaries limit safe and appropriate sexual behavior and offer choices about with whom you interact sexually. They also inform you as to what is and is not acceptable to you. Some partners of sex addicts find they can't acknowledge their sexuality and choose to be nonsexual. If left unattended to, this can lead to denial and a suppression of an important part of being human. Meeting your sexual needs either alone or with another is a choice. Choices can be temporary or fixed.

4. **Relationship** boundaries define the limits of appropriate interaction with others.

5. **Intellectual** boundaries provide the opportunity to enjoy learning and teaching and allow you to be curious and inspired.

6. **Physical** boundaries set limits around touch and space.

Where do you need better boundaries today? If you are not in a relationship, focus on primary friendships, work relationships, or family as you move through each category. With each of the following boundaries you will see examples of how the boundary pertains to you, to your partner, and to someone outside of your relationship. Give an example of how you identify your need for healthier boundaries in each situation.

## EXAMPLES

### Emotional

**Me**: *I recognize that at times my feelings can get overwhelming and I can act too hastily to make them go away. I will have more patience with whatever I feel and allow myself a certain time frame in which to acknowledge my feelings and then move to a new activity.*

**Us**: *I allowed myself to be convinced that your feelings were more important than mine. I will practice telling you what I feel by asking first not to be interrupted. I will do the same for her as well.*

**Other**: *I can struggle not to take on my sister's feelings about her work situation. I would be so worried about it that I couldn't sleep at night. I realize that I don't have to fight her battle and I am learning to listen and validate her pain. This feels a lot different.*

### Spiritual

**Me**: *My faith is my own, no one else's. I will allow others to share in my spiritual practices, but not try to convince them that my way is better than theirs.*

**Us**: *I recognize that your path is very different and that in the past I would try and coerce you into believing like I do. I ask that we find a mutual path we can share together since spirituality is central to both our lives.*

**Other**: *I will stay true to my inner self and not be swayed by my family who wishes I were more like them. By staying honest, I convey my authenticity and recognize their attempts to control are about them and not me.*

### Sexual

**Me**: *I have been so asexual since this all happened. I see that there are other ways I can be attentive to my sexuality. I am going for massages and taking a lot of baths and talking about my fears with my recovery friends.*

**Us**: *I had agreed to an abstinence contract and now that it is over, I need for us to be honest about our intentions when we do have sex, and if either of us is uncomfortable, then we agree to stop. No questions asked.*

**Other**: *My sexual needs are for my partner exclusively, and if that relationship were to end, then I would redefine my boundary based on if I were to start dating.*

### Relationship

**Me**: *I stop and ask myself what it is I want and need before I react to someone else's needs. The outcome is that my needs are more apt to be met if I know what they are.*

**Us**: *I recognize that my recovery is mine and yours is yours; I cannot take responsibility for another person's desires or behaviors. This frees me up to focus on me and allows you to be accountable for you.*

**Other**: *I will no longer be in relationships where I am giving more than I am receiving. I have been drawn to needy and demanding friends and I now recognize I deserve mutuality and respect.*

*I have taken a lot from my friends as a way to avoid being alone. I will watch for that tendency in myself and if I am uncertain will ask if I am pushing him or her away.*

### Intellectual

**Me**: *I will pursue my educational goals even if they are not the ones that others choose for me. I will not accept being called stupid any longer.*

**Us**: *I ask us to address our issues about it not being okay to make a mistake—and work on accepting our imperfections as a part of who we are.*

**Other**: *I am no longer going to accept my father putting me down for decisions I make. I will tell him I need him to stay out of this part of my life. I will tell him I think he means well, but these are my decisions to make and not for his approval or for us to negotiate.*

### Physical

**Me**: *I will eat right and exercise three times a week. I will also dance to music when I want to play.*

**Us**: *We will agree on our individual needs for touch and be willing to acknowledge and accommodate. If either of us feels unavailable or not in a good place to do so, we will speak up.*

**Other**: *I will be aware of how comfortable I really am when others want to hug me and be willing to tell them if I am uncomfortable with such touch.*

Establishing healthy boundaries is vital to your recovery. They are limits on how others can treat you, and by having boundaries you reinforce your self-worth, honor your inner voice, and validate your autonomy. Boundaries provide a framework that will help with your commitment to self to be respected and treated fairly by others. Having boundaries can have an enormous impact on your life, and like learning any new skill, it requires a lot of practice. In early recovery, boundary-setting can seem confusing as you try to find what is and is not tolerable for you. While you may find it difficult to learn new ways to respect yourself, doing so may be one of the greatest gifts in recovery.

Begin with the easiest boundaries first and recognize what are bigger challenges ahead and pace yourself accordingly. It's okay if you are not ready to establish boundaries right away in every area where you know they are needed. Developing and maintaining boundaries will become more familiar and automatic as your self-worth and confidence grow. Take this a step at a time and in a short time you will look behind you and see how far you have come in recovery because you now have a skill set called Healthy Boundaries.

## Decision to Stay or Leave

*"Shall I stay or leave" is a question that most partners ask themselves. You may be quick to answer one way or the other, or you fluctuate in confusion as to what you desire. We recognize that this is a question that is often asked not just at the time of immediate crisis, but for many as the road to recovery has begun. This exercise is intended to sort out the questions to consider if you are undecided whether it is time to stay or leave the relationship.*

Being at the crossroads of deciding whether you should stay or leave the relationship is a difficult one. There is never an easy juncture in which to consider a significant decision such as this, especially if children and socioeconomic concerns are involved. However, there will come a time in your recovery, after a year or perhaps two to three years, when the need to decide becomes more apparent. This is likely to occur when you are able to more realistically assess the relationship in its entirety. Weighing the decision often means looking at the pros and cons of staying with your partner, while considering your fluctuating emotions about him or her, and whether there is a probable chance that things will change for the better.

Considering this choice is different from when you first faced the crisis of sex addiction. At that time, you were reeling from the betrayal and the loss of trust in the relationship. During your healing process of reconstructing what happened and regaining your footing, you confronted fears about your safety, whether your partner was going to act out and/or stay in treatment, and what you were going to do to take care of yourself. As the crisis has receded, you have gained a better grasp of who you are and what you need, and better appreciate what is required for a relationship to grow. These developing insights about yourself make you better prepared to confront the direction you'd like to see the relationship go. If you are undecided whether it is time to stay or leave the relationship, this exercise will sort out the questions to consider.

How do you know this is the time to decide?

**EXAMPLES**

*I am tired of not knowing where my life is going. We both are ready to move ahead with our lives and decide if we should stay together. He's made a lot of changes, but I wonder if the damage is too great for me to continue. We've decided to enter couples' therapy to work on this decision together with a professional.*

· · · ·

*I am still angry at her a lot of the time. I see she is working hard on her program but feel she doesn't have any idea of the pain she has put me through. Unless I see a change in how she treats me emotionally, I feel I need to move on.*

• If you have decided to stay, have you been able to ascertain what it is that makes it possible for you to do so?

## ASSESSING CHANGES

As you are making this decision, it is important to assess any changes that have occurred since the beginning of the recovery process.

• Has he or she changed? Describe.

• Is he or she committed to recovery? Is he or she somewhere in between? How is his or her level of commitment affecting you?

**EXAMPLES**

*I am reassured by it.*

. . . .

*I am anxious since I hear other addicts are more committed than mine and I wonder if she's going to act out again.*

• Is he or she transparent with his or her schedule, time, and the questions you ask?

**EXAMPLES**

*Yes! That was one of the first signs I saw six months into the process. I was no longer having to guess if he was going to make it on time to the kids' events, as he's home beforehand asking if he can take the kids and give me a break.*

. . . .

*I ask a lot of questions, but not as many as in the beginning. Before I could see that she would get upset that she might not be telling me enough and panic. Now I notice that she slows down, breathes deeply, and if she's anxious she'll ask if we can take a break and come back and talk later that day. Then she tells me she made some calls within her program to help in being direct with her answers to my questions. It feels a lot different now.*

• Are you seeing efforts on his or her part to consider your needs on a consistent basis? Is he or she more available with his or her time with you or other shared responsibilities?

**EXAMPLE**

*That was never a problem in our relationship. What I notice now is that when he's with me doing an activity together, he's no longer distracted by other women on the street, looking at his cell phone, or running to check his email on the computer. I feel less anxious when we're together.*

• Have you been able to ask for your nonnegotiables to be met? If so, what has happened?

**EXAMPLE**

*It was so hard for me! But I really believed I had a right to the requests I was making of her and was prepared to act if she wasn't going to work with me. She didn't like it, but she also said she recognized that she'd hurt me and if this is what I needed, then she was willing to do it. That just never would have happened in the past.*

- Are you finding you are able to bring up concerns, questions, and/or fears without receiving defensive responses, withholding information, or behavior and/or excuses? Describe.

## DEVELOPING INTIMACY: REASONS TO STAY

Understanding what has changed means assessing what skills and tools are being used by both of you to cultivate a healthier relationship.

From the list that follows, write down those items that you believe are occurring now in the relationship.

- We are committed to our relationship as long as we both stay in recovery.
- We are addressing emotional and sexual intimacy as a recovering couple.
- We both are able to ask for what each of us needs and feel heard.
- We respect each other consistently.
- We acknowledge the pain that still exists and are committed to giving each other the space needed to continue to heal.
- We believe that honesty is a cornerstone of our relationship in recovery.
- We reach out to others in our support network when an issue stumps us.
- Having our support network is extremely important to our recovery.
- We both commit to having more shared time alone than in the past.
- We laugh.
- We are developing a more equal relationship with shared responsibilities.
- We enjoy each other's company.
- Other.

## INDICATORS: WHEN IT IS TIME TO LEAVE

Partners who confront this decision have often given recovery a chance to take hold, but have found that chronic slips, relapses, or too much damage from the addiction has been done, and they no longer have hope for the relationship. They choose to end it and are prepared to address the loss of doing so. Many find freedom in making this decision and letting go of the ambiguity and fear that has become commonplace.

What changed recently that has you feeling this is a time to decide?

**EXAMPLE**

*I told myself that if my husband slipped again after we had paid for inpatient treatment that I wanted the relationship to end. I had given recovery—both of ours—a chance and inpatient was a bottom line for me. If he could not stay in recovery after having been away for two months to work on his issues, then I could no longer wait for him to change. This was a commitment I made to myself as well as to him. I can't go back to what it's been like.*

- What do you stand to lose (both the good and the bad) if you are to separate? Consider emotionally, financially, spiritually, and socially. What do you stand to gain, including both the good and the bad?

## IF YOU ARE UNDECIDED

Perhaps you know you should leave but are not prepared to do so. There are various reasons to feel this way, but sometimes they are ways to avoid making a decision or justifying reasons for staying or leaving. Consider some steps to help you in this process.

- Describe the conflict you feel.

- What is blocking you from moving forward in the way you wish? What do you believe would help you in working through these roadblocks?

**EXAMPLE**

*Going back to my nonnegotiables list and seeing what I can no longer tolerate and if it occurs again (his contacting the lover), I will move into a separate bedroom.*

• Who do you believe could help you in this process?

**EXAMPLE**

*Being accountable to my therapist and my best friend. Starting to imagine and preparing to have the bedroom to myself would feel good too.*

## SELF-WORTH ISSUES

Sometimes the motivation and drive to make any decision about your relationship is based on your self-perceptions. Recognizing the negative ways you view and treat yourself is necessary for overcoming the roadblocks that stand in the way of you making choices.

• No one else would want me.

• I keep hoping he'll change and if he does I don't want someone else to reap the rewards of that.

• This is as good as it gets.

• I feel too weak to make any decisions.

• I feel there is no way out.

• I am scared about the future.

• Other.

If how you view yourself is playing a big role in getting unstuck, then this is a sign that you can't do this on your own and need professional help. Sometimes the negative messages that stem from childhood are hard to change by yourself. Taking steps to talk about this issue will help you change the old messages and invite in new ones.

Recovery is a process. Unless your welfare or the welfare of your children is at stake, focus on what you need to help you with your conflict. Many partners find they have other emotional issues that emerge as a result of learning about themselves and they feel worse as they move through their healing process. The energy for making a decision about the relationship may be going to other needs you have right now, so slow down the demands you are placing on yourself and put time into what you need to do to get better.

# Rebuilding Healthy Intimacy

*In this section, you have an opportunity to look at the dynamics of being in harmony with another. We discuss ten qualities of an intimate relationship: Respect, Honesty, Realistic Expectations, Trust, Autonomy, Shared Power, Long-term Commitment, Tenderness, Time, and Forgiveness. We ask that you take a moment to reflect on how this relates to you presently, and then we ask you to develop a personal contract with yourself to reinforce your most important needs in an intimate relationship.*

For relationships to function optimally requires both individuals to give fully of themselves. This is also known as emotional attunement. Attunement is defined as *being or bringing into harmony; a feeling of being at one with another human being.* (dictionary.com)

Qualities that reflect attunement are:

**1. Respect**: Respect is an attitude for which courtesy is an expression.

**EXAMPLE**
*My respect is an acceptance of who you are, your autonomy, the uniqueness of you. I expect the same from you toward me. It starts with self-respect.*

Is respect for yourself and your partner something you have or something you would need to work on? Explain.

Active addiction erodes respect in relationships as lies, secrecy, and violating commitments become the fuel for maintaining duplicitous behaviors. Being the recipient of this behavior makes it equally difficult to feel respectful toward a partner who has hurt you. With recovery this can readily change. Assessing changes in your partner or any other relationship means asking yourself, "Does his or her behavior indicate his or her respect for me?" Someone who lies, keeps secrets, or continually breaks promises does not respect you. Someone who can admit his or her faults, take responsibility for harms caused, and show consistent measurable change in his or her actions is developing respectful behavior.

**2. Honesty**: Honesty means truthfulness, sincerity, and speaking from a place of integrity.

EXAMPLE

*I no longer fear I will be rejected for being less than perfect, being vulnerable, or when I disagree with you. I can tell you my feelings and/or my thoughts without fear our relationship will be in jeopardy.*

Obviously in order to be able to do this, you need to first be honest with yourself so you can be honest with another. For some this also means you may need to learn healthy communication skills, the ability to speak for yourself and the ability to listen.

- Is being honest with yourself something you need to work on? Explain.

- To what degree do you trust that your partner is honest with you? Explain.

**3. Realistic Expectations**: No one person is capable of meeting all your needs at all times. Should somebody always be compatible with you, it is very likely he or she hasn't fully developed his or her own sense of self and is fearful of disagreement.

EXAMPLE

*I expect to be called when you plan to come home later than you said. If there is a change in time, I expect a call telling me this.*

- Would you describe your expectations to be unrealistic or realistic? Explain.

**4. Trust**: Means a person feels safe with another person, psychologically and physically. Trust is demonstrated in a person's consistency, predictability, reliability, and following through with intentions. What that person says he or she will do, he or she does. Trust is earned and develops over time. It is not a given.

EXAMPLE

*I feel secure in our relationship and feel respected by you.*

- Would you describe yourself as trustworthy? Are there ways is which you trust too easily or are too fearful to trust at all? Explain.

- In your relationship today, how is your partner demonstrating trustworthiness or is this an area where significant doubts and concerns persist? Explain.

**5. Autonomy**: Means taking full responsibility for your own life, for evolving into the best human being you can be, fulfilling your own life scripts, and exercising your own physical, emotional, mental, and spiritual energies. With autonomy, trust is within, i.e., "I will not forsake myself." With autonomy, you have the ability to be clear about your own needs, being respectful to the boundaries and limits of others as well as your own.

EXAMPLE

*I know my partner and I differ on many issues, but I am learning to find my voice and stand up for my beliefs.*

Be careful. What sometimes passes for autonomy is unbridled, unmitigated selfishness. "To hell with the rest of the world, I am going to get what I want when I want it because I am entitled to do what I please." That is not true. No one is entitled to get what he or she wants when he or she wants it from anyone. That is selfishness, intrusiveness, and greed.

Intimacy means that you have a loving relationship with another person wherein you offer and are offered validation and understanding. You are understood and experience a sense of being valued intellectually, emotionally, and physically. The more you are willing to share, the greater the degree of intimacy. Spiritually and emotionally, intimacy is a sharing of autonomy.

- Would you describe your relationship today as shared autonomy or is it more symbiotic (enmeshed) or severely autonomous (disconnected)? Explain.

- What is needed on your part for your relationship to be more about shared autonomy?

**6. Shared Power**: A healthy relationship is about shared power, not control. Both partners are able to take initiative and to respond. They are able to stand side by side. There is a mutual give and take, reciprocity, and negotiation. A healthy relationship is not a power struggle. The two of you do not have to think or feel the same way about all things. Nor does it mean someone is always right and the other wrong, even if both parties feel convinced of their positions. Sometimes it's about "agreeing to disagree" while acknowledging the other's feelings. A healthy relationship is not symbiotic.

**EXAMPLE**

*In many ways I find it refreshing to disagree with my partner. Since we have been going to therapy, he doesn't seem to take our disagreements so personally.*

- How would you describe "shared power" in your relationship? Does power feel like control, mutually shared, or "one-up, one-down?"

- What do you think you can do to increase shared power?

**7. Long-term Commitment**: Both partners need to value and take seriously the responsibility to the relationship. This means fidelity, faithfulness, respect, and care for the other in good and bad times. Sometimes after recovery, the commitment is simply to each day.

Commitment does not mean staying in a relationship no matter what. Commitment isn't a life sentence. It's a choice that may get challenged. People change, relationships are renegotiated. When you make a commitment, you do what you can to make the relationship work, not allowing yourself to be abused or giving up your integrity in the process. You trust that the two of you together will work this out.

**EXAMPLE**

*My commitment to our relationship is based on both of us actively being engaged in recovery practices.*

What are your thoughts about what it means to make a long-term commitment?

**8. Tenderness**: Tenderness is demonstrated with physical affection. This is the kind of nonsexual physical touching everyone needs to thrive. It is the nurturing touch that says, "I am here, you are not alone." "I offer my support." "Hello." Tenderness is also expressed in words and attitude. It is so easy, after being with a partner for a long period of time, for these niceties to go lax. Sometimes we are willing to offer tenderness to those we don't know, but can neglect our partner. It is easy over time to take our partners for granted.

The dynamics that create emotionally and spiritually safe sex also create physically safe sex. In other words, when you have an intimate adult-to-adult relationship built around spiritually and emotionally healthy guidelines, then physical sex becomes the culminating experience that binds the two of you together.

**EXAMPLE**

*I appreciate your willingness to hold me without the expectation for sex.*

- Is tenderness something you are comfortable giving? How about receiving?

- How has that need changed since disclosure/discovery?

- What do you believe you can to do change this today?

9. **Time**: Valued relationships need time. People can grow apart because they don't see the relationship as its own separate entity requiring time and attention—essential ingredients for it to grow and for the individuals to feel loved, nurtured, and sustained by it. Some people allow themselves to get caught up in other responsibilities and not take the time to *be* in the relationship.

### EXAMPLE

*If my relationship is going to work, I need to spend more quality time with my partner and not so much with my coworkers.*

- How much time do you spend with your partner during the week? Speak in terms of minutes and hours. Do not include sleep.

- What are you doing with that time? How would you like it to be different?

10. **Forgiveness**: There needs to be room for forgiveness. That does not mean forgetting. It means remembering and letting go. It means cleansing yourself of pain and anger. Many people, in order to have peace, are quick to forgive. Forgiveness does not mean selling your heart and soul or your integrity to have peace. It means maintaining your integrity while being able to let go.

### EXAMPLE

*I'm still so hurt and don't want to forgive her, but I know that our relationship won't stand a chance if I don't open my heart to forgiveness.*

- Do you think there is room in this relationship for forgiveness on your part? Explain.

In order to have a healthy relationship, you have to come to terms with the damage done to a relationship impacted by sex addiction. You and the addict must be mutually on board to do the necessary work required to rebuild the relationship. Timing is key. One of you may be further along in your recovery than the other. If you are no longer in the relationship, knowing what constitutes healthy intimacy is important for any relationship that you may enter in the future.

As you consider the ingredients needed for an emotionally attuned relationship, first consider the responsibility to yourself. You are now the gatekeeper of what you will and will not allow and developing a contract helps to reinforce this responsibility to you. Go through the list of qualities for a healthy, attuned relationship listed previously and write what you believe are your most important needs in an intimate relationship.

**EXAMPLE**
Personal contract with myself: *I need _____ and in order for that to occur I need to _____. If in a relationship I would like my partner to _____.*

Now as you reflect on what you have written and expressed as true for you, write what you will no longer accept.

**EXAMPLE**
*I will no longer accept disparaging comments or evasive answers to questions.*

If you are recommitting to the relationship it is important to define what it is you will need for it to be sustained. The following examples describe what has worked for partners of sex addicts in defining a healthy relationship. By defining the terms of the relationship you too can establish boundaries where you can safely explore intimacy.

**EXAMPLES**
*Linda was divorced from a sex addict who didn't stop his acting-out behavior. When she began dating, she explored what she would need in order to feel safe with someone new. First she noted that she needed someone who was trustworthy, reliable, and consistent with his*

*dates. She also was terribly afraid of financial problems since this caused serious trouble in her past relationship.*

· · · ·

*John was deeply hurt and didn't know if he would ever trust Beth again after she had cheated on him for seven years. However, when her recovery became central and consistent over time, he found that his love for her was rekindled. They set about redefining the relationship, since in the past it had been marred by her addiction. Everything that he thought he needed he had to reevaluate, and risk asking for again from the same person who had hurt him before. This was very scary for him, but if he wanted to be with Beth he knew he'd have to be open to trying again. Only this time, he renegotiated aspects of the relationships with his eyes wide open and he had a plan that if she didn't follow through, he would back away and reevaluate his commitment again. Today after three years, their commitment is strong and both are openly able to address fears, hopes, and dreams that previously they kept to themselves.*

Believing and working toward a loving committed relationship becomes more possible when you identify important characteristics of intimacy and act in ways that reflect your values and goals. Having the necessary tools will allow you to practice and sustain positive emotional attunement with others.

## Internal Roadblocks to Recovery

*It is common to experience resistance in your recovery no matter how much you would like to do things differently. The exercises in this section will also help you recognize the source of resistance, encouraging you to be aware of what your concerns or fears may be. This section offers a list of tools that leads you toward healthy change.*

How do you know if you are not moving forward in your recovery? Sometimes in recovery it is common to encounter internal resistance to change. This is understandable, as change is difficult. The barriers are often related to fears about taking the next step forward. Perhaps you have hit a roadblock because you are afraid to confront some aspect of yourself. It is important to trust this place and instead of trying to push through it, recognize there is meaning in this pain that has yet to be revealed. Be patient and gentle with yourself as you work to overcome this plateau.

Here are some examples of partners' experiences:

*One woman kept hoping her husband would engage in treatment despite evidence to the contrary. He wasn't interested in recovery and refused to attend twelve-step meetings. He was evasive with her as to his time and simply told her "it" was over whenever she asked if he was acting out. Her preoccupation meant that her focus on him isolated her from facing the truth that he had no interest in changing. When confronted by others who knew her situation, she admitted that she just didn't want to look at the relationship for what it was.*

· · · ·

*Another woman recalled how difficult it was for her to recognize that her husband was getting better because that meant she'd have to consider letting go of her anger and suspicions. She wanted power over him because she was afraid to be hurt again if she let down her wall.*

· · · ·

*One man found he couldn't stand to be around people and now that he is in recovery he dreads facing what is behind this issue. His growing self-awareness made him recognize that isolation and numbing behaviors like watching TV and playing games on the Internet were contributing to his depressive symptoms.*

## ADAPTATION TO RESISTANCE

Addressing your roadblocks means identifying how the resistance is manifesting itself. Common forms of resistance include:

**Denial:** Only addressing aspects of the addiction while ignoring other destructive elements. *He still acts out, but he's going to SA meetings.*

**General malaise/grief and loss:** Sense of futility—why bother moving forward? *Look at how much I've already lost.*

**Other-centered/excessive business**: Over-focus on the addict, children, work and not enough on your own healing. *I don't have the time to think about this recovery stuff because my work schedule is too demanding.*

**Self-protection**: Being compartmentalized. Not seeing recovery as all encompassing and therefore certain areas of your life remain stuck and resistant to change. *I escape through my books and my computer games so I don't have to think or feel.*

**Addictive behaviors:** Self-defeating and destructive behaviors are distractions from the underlying issues. *My shoplifting has been my way of distracting me from all the changes I may have to make in my marriage.*

Have you found yourself resisting areas of your recovery? If so describe.

**EXAMPLES**

*I found myself trying to make it okay that my spouse wasn't working on his recovery. I didn't want to ask questions about whether he was acting out or not. Then I learned he spent a lot of our savings without telling me and I was faced again with my fear of what to do. I spend a lot of time staying busy so I don't have to face these fears of mine.*

. . . .

*I notice I get lost in my sadness. Sometimes I spend too much time ruminating on everything I've lost and can't seem to find relief from the pain. I tell myself I should be grateful for my kids and my job, but those things just don't matter when I'm feeling this way. I don't reach out to let anyone know how sad I am.*

Whichever form your resistance takes often it's driven by an effort to defend against feelings you wish to avoid or situations that are unacceptable to you. The desire to distance parts of yourself that you dislike is understandable but can lead to unsafe behavior. As a way to increase your awareness and willingness to address those barriers to your recovery consider the following.

- If I were to give more attention to my internal experiences, I am concerned that I _____ .

- I have mixed feelings about looking at my resistance. They include _____ .

- What might I gain if I overcome my roadblocks?

- What am I willing to do in the meantime to continue looking at my resistance?

Let's step back to a time when you felt more certain about a challenging situation. It may be when you got your first job or applied to school or when you became a parent and had to make some choices in how to handle things you never before encountered.

- Describe a time in your life when you were able to confront an unwelcome situation in your life.

- What did you learn about yourself from that experience?

- What attribute(s) and/or coping skill(s) did you have at the time that helped you overcome that situation?

Steps to take to address impediments to change are

- Identify;
- Acknowledge;
- Accept.

Tools to use as you work toward healthy change are

- Engage in dialogue with yourself; assess your thoughts, feelings, and desired outcome to the situation that is troubling you.

- Talk to others whom you trust.

- Journal about it as a way to further the exploration of your thoughts and feelings and desired outcome and look for any new ideas and possible solutions to the situation.

- Challenge your thinking; become flexible. Part of resisting change is being inflexible.

- Pay attention to your internal voice: use affirming, compassionate statements, such as, "I can push though this fear," "I am making changes at my own pace and time," and "I have the tools available that I need to get through this situation."

- Question and consider options: "If I do this, then will this happen?"

If you are struggling to face roadblocks that are inhibiting you, what words/ statements could you say to yourself to help you along the way? Write five statements of your own.

A balanced, yet nurturing voice is most effective in influencing change. It keeps you centered on the task at hand and provides comfort along the way.

**EXAMPLES**

*I know this is a difficult time, but I believe in me.*

• • • •

*I only have to do the next right thing.*

To face your internal roadblocks means you are on the path to increasing your self-awareness. However, this brings with it risk—the risk of changing and becoming more authentic as you recognize and face your fears. By addressing unwanted and previously avoided feelings while adopting new coping behaviors, you benefit by becoming more true to yourself and open yourself to having greater freedom and autonomy.

## Reconstructing Sexuality

*This section gives you the opportunity to think about your relationship with sex. When in a relationship where there has been sexual betrayal and a lack of healthy boundaries regarding sex, sexual esteem is greatly impacted. You will have the opportunity to find direction as to what you want to focus on in your recovery sexually and answer questions for yourself that help you look at your motivation for being sexual. Lastly, it reinforces allowing your sexual life to be in tune with your value system.*

When you have been subject to sexual betrayal there is often confusion about your own sexuality. You may have felt good about your sexuality at one time in your life but are now confused as to what is pleasing, what is safe, and how you trust the relationship of sharing this part of who you are. Then again, it is possible that your sexuality is something that has always been a source of conflict or pain for you. Aside from the betrayal felt through sexual deception, you are also a part of a highly sexualized society, where the media, culture, and family gives many mixed messages about sexuality.

Many men and women who have experienced repeated sexual infidelities have had to confront the loss of their sexuality as they knew it, feeling it has been contaminated and tainted by the behaviors of their partner. Their sense of sexual safety is shaky at best. Healing from the wreckage of addiction understandably takes time and effort. Believing the addict alone needs to change in order to feel safe, trusting, and to feel sexually alive is a falsehood, and you may need to change if you are to get better. Your sexuality is your own and whatever the consequences the sexual deception have brought you can stop if you believe you have the right to choose what is healthy for you.

First and foremost, you need to have the ingredients of greater intimacy to have a sexual life that goes beyond the physical expressions of sex. You also need to have a sense of what sex means to you and to feel good about yourself sexually before you are in a position to enjoy healthy sexuality.

The following exercise is a good place in which to initially give some thought about your own relationship with sex. Take a look at the list below and write down all of the words that describe how you experience sex in your life. Then write all of the words that describe how you would *like* to experience sex.

| | | |
|---|---|---|
| Angry | Guilt-free | Pleasurable |
| Awkward | Honest | Relaxed |
| Bad | Hurtful | Respectful |
| Exciting | Intimate | Rough |
| Playful | Safe | Frisky |
| Satisfying | Forceful | Overpowering |
| Secretive | Shame-free | Shameful |
| Spiritual | Spontaneous | Nonexistent |
| Other | | |

- What differences do you see between how you experience sex and how you would like to experience sex?

Healthy sexuality is an inherent part of who you are. It is shaped and defined by family, society, and your individual preferences. To develop sexually in a healthy manner means you are able to choose with whom, where, and how you wish to be sexual. You decide which sexual practices interest you or not. Healthy sexuality is free of coercion and power and is something developed over time. Healthy sexuality is operating from a place of respect for yourself and others. Healthy sexuality

- Accepts the imperfect.
- Adds to self-esteem.
- Has no victims.
- Holds integrity.
- Is fun and playful.
- Maintains respect.
- Relies on safety.

Healing your sexual self often begins with insight about how your earlier influences have impacted your sexual being. Reflect on the following questions:

- What did you witness between your parents regarding affection and sex? What were their attitudes towards sex? Were you given any specific messages regarding masturbation, sex outside of marriage, the purpose of sex, etc.?

- Were you ever sexually abused? If so, did you ever tell anyone? How was it addressed?

- Were there any specific cultural messages you heard that have influenced your thoughts and feelings about your sexuality and the role of sex in relationships?

- To what degree has media influenced your beliefs about being sexual?

- Have there been any friends or significant others who you think are/have been important in your developing sexuality? In what way have they been important to how you feel about yourself sexually or your specific beliefs?

When you consider your sexual self-esteem, where do you stand on the statements below? In your journal write down your answer after each statement.

**I am sexually appealing.**

Strongly Disagree

Disagree

Unsure

Agree

Strongly Agree

**I have confidence in my ability to have sex in a satisfying and enjoyable way.**

Strongly Disagree

Disagree

Unsure

Agree

Strongly Agree

**I am comfortable with my sexual self-esteem at this time.**

Strongly Disagree

Disagree

Unsure

Agree

Strongly Agree

**I know what I like and don't like during sex.**

Strongly Disagree

Disagree

Unsure

Agree

Strongly Agree

**I am able to communicate my sexual likes and dislikes during sex.**

Strongly Disagree

Disagree

Unsure

Agree

Strongly Agree

• What are your thoughts at this time about being sexual?

## REENGAGING SEXUALLY

Partners often ask about the risks of reengaging sexually. It is important to ask yourself whether or not you are acting within your own value system and whether or not believe you can choose to be sexual and how. Consider what your safety concerns are and express them to your partner beforehand. Sex will feel different in recovery. It will require willingness to change and openness to explore new ideas, both your own and your partner's.

Reengaging sexually is bound to elicit many conflicting feelings. It is important to know your motivations for being sexual and to be sure you are acting in your own best interests. Ask yourself:

• Do I want to be sexual out of fear that he or she will go elsewhere if I am not?

• Do I think I will be able to control his or her behavior if I am sexual with him or her?

• Do I believe having sex reaffirms he or she still loves me?

• Do I withhold sex as a way of punishing him or her?

• Do I not want to be sexual because I don't sense the intimacy sex would imply?

The following situations are areas in which you need to be more vigilant to ensure healthier sexuality. By being more aware, you are more present with yourself and are in a better position to make decisions about how available you are to being sexual with your partner.

• If you feel that he or she is distracted and not being present.

• If sex is a reaction to a fight and being used to replace discussion of an uncomfortable topic.

• If having sex is not consensual.

- If you feel manipulated.

- If you are asked to engage in unwanted sexual acts or fantasies.

- If you mistake intensity for love.

- If you do not enjoy it.

- If you feel any shame or lack of respect from your partner during the act.

Are there other safety concerns you need to have respected if you are to engage sexually?

We strongly encourage you to read more about healthy sexuality. And certainly, the expression of your sexuality is directly related to the safety, respect, and integrity of the relationship. Your sexuality is an important part of who you are, but it is a part, not the whole. Healthy expression of sexuality is about choice. You have choices about the person(s) with whom you are sexual and the manner in which you express that sexuality. It is critical that as you engage with another, you have interdependence, "I am giving myself to you, but I am not losing myself to do so." You also have choices about self-stimulation as well as abstinence. These choices are dynamic, meaning that while you are grounded in your self-respect, how you experience your own sexuality can be expressed differently in the many passages throughout your life.

## Concerns for Children

*For those of you who are parents and ask, "What about the kids?"—this section is for you. After a brief discussion about the impact on children you will identify the ways you think your children are affected. While there are many feelings involved, putting this down on paper makes it more real and more feasible for you to address your concerns. Asking you to take responsibility where you can, we also offer guidance on the parenting practices that support resiliency in your children. Then there is the tough question about what to say to your kids. While that varies according to each child and situation, there are some basics to consider that we will discuss. This is a tender subject, but you have shown much courage to get to this point. Draw on your strengths and be the best parent you can be.*

There comes a time in this process when you say, "What about the kids?" You may be concerned about whether or not and to what degree they are affected by this behavior or what it is they should be told. Everyone's situation is different, but first and foremost you need to keep the needs of the children up front. Whether they are young or adult age, you need to be the best parent you can be.

## THE IMPACT ON CHILDREN

Whether or not they are aware of the sexual acting out, children are much more affected by the family dynamics than you may realize. This may be evident in their relationship with the addict. Your child may show distance, resentment, and hurt toward the addict due to years of physical absences and not showing up to events important to the child, as well as being subjected to lies and broken promises. The addict may overcompensate out of guilt and shame, which is unsettling to the child who doesn't know what to make of his or her parent who alternates in being uninterested and then indulgent with gifts or attention.

Your behavior and how you and the child's other parent are relating to each other has a direct impact. Your anger, depression, using the child to communicate for you or not allowing the child to be autonomous, or using him or her as your confidant or friend will create long-term problems. The hurt that children experience is just as often about the unhealthy expression of emotions and poor relational skills as it may be about sexual messages they internalize due to the sexual acting out.

When children sense or know that there is marital betrayal, which they often do, they are confused, angry, and are inevitably caught in the middle of you and the other parent due to their loyalty to each of you. If there is public exposure of the sexual behaviors, then that creates another level of reactions and consequences for the children.

### EXAMPLES

*I saw my mother with this other man and I didn't know what to say to her or my father.*

· · · ·

*I learned from a friend that she saw my mother with another man at a park near our school. This was after I saw nude pictures of her on her cell phone. I am so angry and embarrassed!*

Socially, children are affected. They may have to move due to the marital crisis, or they may be restricted from friends or extended family due to acting out. Their friendships may suffer as public knowledge exposes them to scrutiny by their peers, or perhaps the child's behavior has changed and this is influencing their relationships. Emotionally, children may become depressed, anxious, fearful, or angry. They may be compensating and cast into a premature adult role with unrealistic responsibilities. This all has the potential to contribute to difficulty with healthy intimacy in their adult lives.

### EXAMPLES

*I don't do relationships at all because I spent years seeing how messed up my parents were.*

. . . .

*There was always a shadow cast over our family. My mom was so upset a lot of the time, and my dad acted like everything was fine. Yet all of us kids knew he was lying to Mom. I wish my mom would have stood up to him. I always wanted to do what I could to make my mom happier because my dad was treating her so badly.*

Children growing up with addiction often vow, "It will never happen to me." Yet when they meet with life's difficulties, they don't have the emotional maturity or coping skills to live their life differently. History has proven that time and time again in the throes of living with addictive behavior, whether or not it is recognized as such, children experience emotional abandonment that sets them up to seek ways to escape or numb their pain, often leading to various manifestations of addiction. They begin to repeat the models they were raised with, while rationalizing, minimizing, and denying that they, too, are a part of the addictive cycle. They act out sexually or become the "perfect" partner. We have seen many parents who have worked incredibly hard to compensate for the behaviors of the addicted parent, and it is very possible your children wouldn't have many of the strengths they have had you not compensated in some way. But you must also recognize how your own emotional disconnection, rigidity, silenced anger, or other specific codependent behaviors have impacted your children.

- Name and identify your children by age. In general, in what ways do you think your children have been impacted?

• More specifically, identify how each of your children may be showing the effects of their parent's addiction.

### EXAMPLES

*I notice my daughter, who found out about her father's addiction at sixteen years old, is still, at twenty-five, unable to sustain a long-term relationship. I think it's because of what went on with her father, but I don't know for sure. I'm afraid to ask her any questions.*

. . . .

*My seven-year-old unfortunately has been exposed more to my behavior since his father is mostly physically absent. Between my severe reactivity and his father's absence I have a child who isolates in his room. When I force him to come out when people are around, he is clingy one moment and having a tantrum the next.*

## PROTECTIVE FACTORS

As you consider the impact on your children, it is important to underscore that your parenting of them goes on. More so than words, in the long run, how you parent will have the greatest effect. Take responsibility where you can. The resiliency of children will be supported when you:

• Keep your children's lives on track.

• Maintain healthy family rituals and traditions.

• Listen attentively.

• Develop healthy boundaries.

• Validate emotions.

• Model and teach problem-solving skills.

• Model healthy ways of coping with stress.

• Protect your children as appropriate.

• Steer your children toward appropriate resources.

• Realize the relationship with your children's other parent is theirs and not yours.

• Engage in your own recovery practices.

- Identify skills and practices you do that you believe contribute to healthy parenting. Then consider how you might build upon this during this time of crisis in the family.

- Identify three behaviors you would like to strengthen to be a healthier parent.

In recovery you will find the strength to be the parent your children need you to be. You will probably always feel sad your children have been exposed to addiction and that your behavior has caused them pain. It is normal to be concerned and fearful of the consequences for your children. With support from others in recovery and with the guidance of skilled helping professionals, you can do your part by taking responsibility and being accountable to your children.

## TALKING TO CHILDREN ABOUT SEX ADDICTION

As much as parents wish to protect children from their own mistakes or hurtful behaviors, keeping secrets does not provide the sought after protection. Both clinical experience and early research indicates that many children, of all ages, already knew or suspected that infidelity was occurring before their parents disclosed it to them. Parents seldom want to share their secrets, their pain, or their betrayal with their children. You don't want your children to suffer; you want to protect them from pain. Yet all members of the family are affected by addiction and codependency. Healthy communication and ongoing recovery practices will make it possible to revisit areas of concern your children may experience about the impact of addiction on their lives.

### EXAMPLES

*I was surprised that my mother was not aware that I knew. I carried this secret with me my entire adolescence.*

. . . .

*I knew. I had read my father's diary. It was quite a shock. I told my best friend, but I never told anyone else.*

. . . .

*Sure I would rather have not known about any of this. I don't think any of us who have had this experience want to know this stuff. But that is impossible because in my case I was living in a house with two addicts, my father a sex addict, and my mother addicted to him.*

Talking to children about the real issues is a much more difficult conversation if the addicted person is continuing to act out or the two of you are simply not in agreement as to what and when to share. Before you disclose to your children, talk to other partners in recovery or a skilled therapist; their experience may prove very helpful as you sort through your specific situation. Whether or not you have the support of the addict, consider the following.

## RATIONALE FOR TALKING TO CHILDREN

There is much to consider when thinking of disclosing to children: their ages, the setting, the timing, who tells them, and how much to tell. Four pertinent reasons to disclose to children are:

1. **Validation**: Having their unspoken perceptions validated takes away the craziness of knowing but not knowing. It diminishes the additional shame and anxiety that comes with secrecy.

2. **Exposure**: Children may find out. Often other family members, particularly a sibling, or other children in the neighborhood or school know and may deliberately or inadvertently tell them. In some cases, children stumble upon information about the behavior by reading about it in a newspaper, on the Internet, or even television. A question to consider is, if they were to find out, would I rather it come from me/us or from the public, friends, or other outside sources?

3. **Safety**: The word "addiction" can mislead some people to believe that a person has no control over any aspect of his or her sexuality. That is not true. Do not automatically equate sex addiction with child molestation. But if your partner has been engaged in child pornography or known to sexually act out with minors, your child is at risk and this warrants asking your children whether or not they have ever been inappropriately asked to do something sexual for or with your partner. But we say this with caution. It is very easy to distort the situation through your outrage and fear. We strongly suggest you allow a qualified, helping professional to assist you in how to handle this discussion, the words to use, and the timing.

4. **Breaking the generational cycle**: An age-appropriate, open, honest discussion and education on the basics of addiction and recovery set the stage for ending the generational repetition that occurs in addictive family systems. Addiction thrives in secrecy, so it is important to model that your family is not keeping shame-based secrets.

## APPROPRIATE AGE

If the children are pre- or early adolescent, issues of the child's safety or exposure to the information via another avenue, such as at school, from a sibling, or in the media are the strongest reasons to talk to them or if there is an imminent separation like residential treatment or one parent living separate from the family. Even though the 2000 study by Black, Dillon, and S. Carnes indicated pre- and early adolescents said they were aware, developmentally their greatest need is a belief in the stability of their family. It is the child's own sense of security that is most challenged at this moment. To have sexual data about a parent prior to mid-adolescence is too confusing for him or her to be able to derive positive meaning or value from having that information. Certainly, maturity varies greatly so the professional involved needs to assess the maturity level. By mid-adolescence, as much as children don't want to be told, being told validates their perceptions and they can better cope with the family stress knowing the information.

## DISCRETIONARY CONVERSATION

You may choose not to share information with your kids about the sexual behaviors of the acting out, but their experiences related to the stress within the family need to be validated and supported. Basic information can easily validate their perceptions.

### EXAMPLES

*My kids were seven and nine when everything came out in the open. They had seen and heard anger and crying, and they were aware their father had been absent a lot. When my husband went to treatment, we simply told the kids that he had done some hurtful things, and he was going to get some help. I thought the best thing I could do for them was to keep a routine to their lives. Their father and I told them that we loved them, that these problems were not about them, and that we were going to try very hard to work things out and have a happy family.*

. . . .

*Your dad has a secret that has hurt me deeply. We are both sad right now and are working hard to fix the problem by being very honest with each other.*

. . . .

*We love you and we are sorry we have not paid attention to you and that we have lashed out at you when we were angry with each other. Yes, we are having some adult problems, but they are not about you. You are precious to us, and we both love you very much.*

A more complete disclosure rather than a partial one may be indicated if your children are adults. Framing the problem directly as problematic sexual behavior, in the long run, is healthier for the family. It offers validation to what they most likely already know; it is better that they hear it from you rather than finding out from others. It may also identify a problem that exists for someone else in the family and set into motion the possibility of stopping the repetition of a family legacy. Lastly, you are modeling that problems, when faced directly, can be addressed. Freeing people from secrets lessens the power of shame.

### EXAMPLE

*As much as I didn't want to tell my three kids who were in their twenties why their father and I were really separated, we did. And within a couple of months, my son told me he was into compulsive masturbation and wanted help. My daughter told me she suspected her boyfriend was secretly engaging in cybersex. Had I not been honest with them I don't know if they would have seen their situations to be problematic so quickly, nor would they have seen me as a resource for help.*

Questions to think about regarding your children:

- What is in the best interest of the child/children?
- What is my motivation for telling them? Is it to hurt my partner, to get support, or for their well-being?
- How is it helpful for him or her or them to have this knowledge?
- How will it be hurtful for him or her or them not to know?

Due to the many variables of the family system, the individual child, and the extent and type of sexual behavior acted out, determination about disclosure must be made on a case-by-case basis.

- Name your children and then identify what the rationale is for talking directly with them or with a more discretionary approach.

- If your children already know the facts, describe how they learned and your feelings about it. You can answer this individually for each child or collectively for all of your children.

As painful as your journey has been, stay focused on the protective factors. Research is telling us that protective factors are more powerful than the vulnerability children are exposed to. Be your best parent!

CHAPTER SIX

# Moving Forward

You probably have already engaged in thoughts about forgiveness, the role of spirituality in recovery, and what your life may look like in the future. Yet until now it has been premature to ask you to examine these thoughts. At this stage we believe you have found greater self-respect and have a stronger sense of yourself, your needs, and your wants. You have begun the grief process and many of you are well into it. All of this lays the foundation for more thoughts about forgiveness.

For some readers, your spiritual path has been the foundation of your strength, for others not, and for still others, somewhere in between. As authors, we encourage you to explore this area of recovery for it may allow you to find greater peace and fortitude. We don't want to tell you what you need to do, but would be remiss in not asking you to explore more deeply at this stage. We also know that you are more apt to move forward when you can look forward. Each of these exercises will take you one more step forward.

## The Question of Forgiveness

*The exercises in this section will help you to explore what forgiveness means to you and whether or not and/or how it fits into your healing process. We also challenge you to look at whether or not you have engaged in forgiveness prematurely, engaging in what is referred to as "false forgiveness." Regardless of where you are with the forgiveness of your partner, we do strongly encourage you to be willing to forgive yourself for any behaviors on your part that have been hurtful to yourself and to others.*

Whether or not the relationship between you and your partner survives, the decision to forgive what happened is a personal one that only you can make. Most partners understandably struggle with whether or not to forgive, what it means to forgive, and more importantly, the timing of when it is appropriate to do so. Forgiveness is a process and begins with acknowledging that you have been wronged and owning the feelings associated with having been harmed by another's actions. It involves engaging in the stages of grief, establishing boundaries, and becoming more certain of what is and is not tolerable for you about the relationship. It is often when the transgressions have been fully realized, accepted, and processed that you find yourself thoughtfully considering the place forgiveness may hold in your recovery.

It may be easier to appreciate what forgiveness is by recognizing what forgiveness is not. The following thoughts may be helpful to you as you sort through your feelings and come to terms with the role forgiveness may serve in your healing.

- Forgiveness is not forgetting what has happened. Past experiences and pain have a great deal to teach you about not being victimized again. Forgiving the people who hurt you does not mean you condone or absolve them of their behavior. You are *not* saying that what was done to you was acceptable or unimportant or was not hurtful. It was important. It happened and it hurt. It has irreparably made a difference in your life. Forgiveness doesn't erase what he or she has done. Your partner is still responsible for the harm his or her behavior has created.

- Forgiveness doesn't mean you are never angry again about what occurred. What happened to you was not right; it was not fair. Significant dates or situations such as an anniversary or a reminder of the acting out are times that your anger may get reactivated.

- Forgiveness doesn't happen by making a one-time decision. No matter how sincerely you want to let go of the past and move on with your life, you cannot just wave a magic wand or flip a switch and blithely make the past disappear in one moment.

- Forgiveness doesn't mean reconciliation. Sometimes you fight against any form of forgiveness because you think that means you have to stay in the relationship or that you made a mistake for leaving it.

Forgiveness is a process of letting go of resentments, preoccupation, and controlling behavior. These actions and emotions no longer have a hold on you as you find yourself relinquishing the past while not forgetting it.

With forgiveness:

- You no longer build an identity around something that happened to you. You realize that there is more to you than your shared history with your partner. The past is put into its proper perspective.

- You recognize that grudges and resentments and your anger and disgust have dissipated. Self-pity has been replaced with self-compassion. You recognize how negative emotions impede your well-being and feel you can now choose not to dwell on them. The impulse to use these emotions as a weapon to hurt those who hurt you or to keep other people from getting close enough to hurt you again has lessened. You no longer want to punish the people who hurt you. Forgiveness is the inner peace you feel when you stop trying to do so.

### EXAMPLE

*Forgiveness took time—time for me to heal, to come to my own rescue, to sort out all the confusion, control, and obsession, and to let go. It also took the help of a counselor. For me forgiveness had many prongs. I had to forgive my parents, my abuser, my husband, and most importantly I had to forgive myself. I had to forgive myself for not being perfect, for not protecting myself, for not getting help and into recovery sooner.*

Forgiveness is about being true to yourself. Forgiveness is something that you come to gradually over time. So don't put a timetable on this or place any unrealistic expectations on yourself.

Are you ready or willing to begin to forgive your partner for his or her behavior?

Yes                No                Unsure

If the answer is "yes" or "unsure," you may find writing a letter using the format in the examples below to be helpful. This is a letter to help you focus on your own healing, not one that is given to your partner. Before you get started, think in terms of parts—what part of his or her behavior can you forgive?

**EXAMPLES**
*Dear _____ ,*
*I want you to know I forgive you for. . .*
*I forgive you for. . .*
*I forgive you for. . .*

Or try,
*I want you to know I am working on forgiving you for. . .*
*I want you to know I am working on forgiving you for. . .*
*I want you to know I am working on forgiving you for. . .*

Just acknowledging that you are working toward forgiveness can give you important insights as to where you are in your grief process, your own sense of stability and safety, and/or whether you are experiencing greater empathy and compassion for your partner.

Once you write this letter, stop and take a deep breath and ask yourself, is this a heartfelt experience or is it more of thinking "I should?"

Much of how you think about forgiveness comes from how it was or was not modeled in your family. It also is strongly influenced by your religious or spiritual teachings.

What are your thoughts and feelings about forgiveness? What expectations do you have about yourself regarding forgiveness?

So often when people want to forgive, they make it a global, generalized gesture. "I forgive you for *all* you have done." To get to such a heartfelt forgiveness, you need to look at the specifics of what you are forgiving.

- Consider the various ways you have felt wronged by the addict. As you reflect on all that occurred, can you identify those acts or situations that would warrant forgiveness?

**EXAMPLES**

*I forgive you for having an affair with my sister.*

. . . .

*I forgive you for taking our daughter with you when you met your boyfriend in the motel.*

. . . .

*I forgive you for exposing me to gonorrhea.*

Because the various transgressions will have different values or meanings attached to them, it is likely you are able to forgive more readily in some areas than others. While it may be overwhelming and unrealistic to acknowledge each and every hurtful behavior, it is nonetheless important to identify the various situations that have the greatest significance to you. In this way, you can evaluate what you are and are not prepared to forgive and not get trapped into believing you have to forgive more than you are able to.

## WHEN FORGIVENESS GOES AWRY

Be cautious though, as you may be apt to readily forgive. If you have a habit of being compliant and go to great lengths to avoid conflict, these are indicators that you might engage in premature or false forgiveness. For many people this is strongly reinforced through their religious teachings, societal, and gender messages. Women in particular are more conditioned than men to be understanding, to not get angry, and to forgive. Prematurely forgiving may also be a sign of a lack of self-respect that has been reinforced in a relationship that is unhealthy. If there is a history of domestic violence or other forms of abuse or neglect, it is highly likely that forgiveness is a topic that will need considerable time and preparedness on your part.

You also may get a lot of pressure from your partner, who realizes you know about his or her acting out behaviors and as a way to circumvent consequences, quickly promises to stop, apologizes profusely, and asks for your forgiveness. What he or she is usually looking for is reassurance that you will not leave, that you still love him or her, and that you won't keep holding it against him or her. It is manipulation; wherein if you say you forgive your partner then that seems to pronounce that there is no more need for questions or discussion. After all, haven't you forgiven him or her? False forgiveness is an act that deepens the denial process by promoting an illusion of closeness when nothing has substantially changed, been faced, or resolved. In an attempt to maintain the relationship, you let go of your self-respect and integrity, sacrificing safety when you do so.

### EXAMPLES

*I thought I forgave my husband. I said the words; I smiled. Of course I knew I was hurt. I was angry, but I was working so hard to not be angry. I thought that made me look bad and I wanted him to be the bad person, after all his behavior was the problem. I just couldn't tolerate being out of control with my feelings, which is how I get when I'm angry. So I smiled and talked forgiveness and then silently punished and controlled him as much as I could. I was still living inside his addiction.*

. . . .

*Prior to my beginning any specific recovery I had a lot of years where I thought I'd forgiven him. Mostly I had gone numb and was struggling to just breathe.*

You won't get to a place of heartfelt forgiveness without being emotionally honest with yourself. When you say you forgive but you have not grieved your pain, not owned the injustice, then you've only partially done the work involved in forgiveness. Most likely there are roadblocks standing in your way that are worth exploring.

Do you think you have engaged in false forgiveness? If yes, describe the times you have engaged in false forgiveness. What did you tell yourself?

If you recognize that you have engaged in false forgiveness, you can own that and then continue to pursue what you need to do in your recovery to get to a place where any forgiveness of your partner is genuine and sincere. But foremost in your recovery you must find the ability to forgive yourself.

## SELF-FORGIVENESS

It is our belief that before you get to true forgiveness of another, you need to first forgive yourself. You need to be as compassionate to yourself as you might be to another, and that means forgiving yourself for any behavior that has hurt others and behaviors that have hurt you. You may have been unavailable to your children or close friends because you were caught up in the throes of the addiction or depression. You may have retaliated for the wrongs done to you by having an affair or seeking out other sex partners. The acts may have been against yourself through negative self-talk, blaming yourself for what went wrong, and not being able to hold him or her accountable for the addiction. You may have lied and covered up for the addict; ignored, minimized, and discounted your perceptions; tolerated abusive behavior; and attempted to make peace at any cost. You are human and you deserve acceptance for who you are in your humanness. Now is the time to show some greater self-compassion for yourself.

### EXAMPLES

*Even more helpful to me in my recovery than coming to forgive my husband was coming to forgive myself. I have been able to forgive myself for how my fears allowed me to stay a doormat, to not confront him when I had concerns he was lying to me, and then how I would back down from my ultimatums. I would berate myself, doubt myself. Oh, I had beaten up myself for so much of my life. It is nice to get to a place where I don't do that anymore and have understanding and compassion for why and how I did those things to myself.*

. . . .

*I have had to forgive myself for a lot of my behavior that was hurtful toward me. A biggie for me was that I felt like I prostituted myself to him in doing sexual things I didn't want to do just to keep him happy or to keep him from getting angry. Today I accept that that behavior came from me being scared and not having a strong sense of my own worth. I don't want to ever be in that place again.*

List those things for which you would like to forgive yourself.

To get to a place of self-forgiveness you begin by stopping your negative self-talk, such as "I should have known better. How could I have been so naive?" Self-recrimination will only make you feel worse. You were scared, operating from a place of low self-worth; you may simply have not known how to protect yourself, to honor yourself, or express your feelings any differently. Further, you were up against a person who willfully withheld information from you and when confronted used manipulative ways to avert being truthful. Recognizing the extent of what you were up against may help you to pause, be reflective, and invite self-compassion for how you responded to this trauma. Self-care, nurturance, and taking baby steps will move you toward self-forgiveness. It won't come at once, but gradually. As your self-worth grows so will freedom from the pain and the heartache.

An exercise that facilitates this self-awareness process is a *Letter to Self*. There are three steps to this letter. Begin with the salutation,

1. Dear Self,

2. Write one to two paragraphs focusing on self-compassion. Example:
   *Dear Self,*
   *You have had a very painful time. It was very confusing. You thought you were living life and then things started to get weird. You didn't really trust yourself and wanted to trust him. You didn't want another relationship to fail.*

3. Take whatever issues you are prepared to think about, identify them, and write statements that reflect a greater understanding and acceptance of yourself. Be careful not to write statements that are judgmental of yourself.

**EXAMPLES**

*Dear Self,*

*When you left the kids alone to go look for her you weren't thinking. Your brain shut down. Of course you love your children, but in that moment your fear of losing her was too much. In your mind all you could see was the threat. Of course you are guilt-ridden and angry with yourself. Yes it was wrong and it could have resulted in something worse, but it is over now. Castigating yourself only makes you feel worse about yourself and doesn't help your children.*

. . . .

*Dear Self,*

*When you agreed to go to a strip club, swap partners, and watch porn movies with him you didn't want to and felt dirty doing so. You were just trying to save your relationship. That is one more example of doing whatever your boyfriend wants and not honoring yourself. So this is a painful lesson, but just a lesson. It doesn't mean you are stupid or immoral; it simply means you didn't love yourself at the time or didn't trust yourself to say no. You were too scared of losing him and this was your way of trying to hold on to him and not feel abandoned by him. You have had a lot of pain in your life so it is understandable you reacted the way you did. Know you are building a stronger self, and you won't ever have to compromise yourself in these ways again. It is okay to stop beating yourself up—just for today.*

When you write this letter, it will tap into feelings of grief. You may find repeating the letter at different times helpful as it may allow you to access other memories and feelings that surface that need validation. Writing may reveal that you are still struggling with forgiveness, or that it frees you as you find release, relief, and greater self-acceptance.

**EXAMPLE**

*I cannot stress enough how important the concept of self-forgiveness and self-love were to me. Until I truly forgave and loved myself, I had no capacity to give the same gift to someone else.*

## The Role of Spirituality

*Now we want you to give thought to how spiritual practice can be a part of your recovery. You may find your faith or spiritual practice has strongly guided you already in your healing or that you feel very conflicted about the role of faith and spirituality at this time in your life. While encouraging you to be open to ways spiritual practice can be of guidance to you, this section does not tell you what spiritual practice is needed, but takes you through a process of being introspective and supporting you in this process.*

Infidelity and all that comes with it doesn't leave you much time or energy for the emotional work required to build or maintain a connection with God or a higher power. You may not be the least bit convinced that a spiritual solution offers you any solace or answers. You may have little practice in allowing God into your life or you may be questioning your faith. Then again, it may be your faith or spiritual practices that have given you the strength to keep going. Faith may be your rock, the foundation from which all else flows.

It's possible your entire life has been about reacting, surviving, and being preoccupied or watchful of other people's behaviors. You've found your worth and value in terms of how others define or see you; you've been trying to please, accommodate, and take care of others. However, self-discovery and introspection cannot be done solely from the outside. Serenity begins with your inner world, not with seeking answers from the outer world you have come to rely upon.

Most partners we have worked with come to find an acceptance and peace in their lives as they embrace some form of spiritual or meditative practice. For some, this is a belief in God or a Higher Power. Some exercise faith in a Higher Being through their religious practice, at their house of worship; others find theirs through involvement with their twelve-step fellowships. Others do this through their relationship to nature, song, or meditation.

Whatever spiritual path you take, whether it's Christianity, Judaism, Islam, or Mother Earth and whatever form it takes—prayer, song, nature, meditation—what's important is that you keep moving forward and growing as you travel along the path you have chosen.

While you may not come from a background where you were introduced to a Higher Power or you were not raised in a family where a specific faith was practiced, we ask that you be open to the possibility. You may have been raised with religion, but have moved away from it and during this time of instability have found comfort going back to those familiar rituals from the past. Conversely, you may have discovered a new spiritual practice that has given you hope and inspiration for the journey ahead. Whatever the path, its purpose is to stimulate and enhance, not stifle, your spiritual well-being.

The men and women we have worked with have taught us that incorporating a spiritual path was essential to their recovery. Without some regular and mindful practices in their lives, the journey was harder, more isolating, and hopeless. The following may help you to explore this possibility for yourself.

If you practice a particular faith or engage in a particular spiritual practice, describe and identify how it supports you in your healing process.

**EXAMPLES**

*My daily meditations help me stay centered on the here and now, and not engage in so much overreaction.*

. . . .

*Meeting with my spiritual leader keeps me grounded in my faith and comforts me when I feel lost. I'm given articles and books to read that have deepened my understanding of my relationship to God and have helped me understand why bad things happen.*

• It is not uncommon that religion and recovery can seem at odds, and introspection and guidance can be especially helpful. Have any of the religious tenets or rules of your faith interfered with your healing? If so, how? What might you do to get help with this conflict?

**EXAMPLE**

*My faith is important to me and it says I need to honor my partner. I have been led to believe that means I can't question my husband, let alone ask for what I need. I fear my church community would be harsh to me if I were to leave him.*

• As a child, were there any particular rituals or ceremonies that were of special value or meaning for you? What were they? Describe how they were meaningful. Do they hold an interest for you today?

EXAMPLES

*As a child, each day I began with a morning prayer. It was simple and it just asked my higher power to be with me that day. We were Christian, so it is God. I think it would be lifting for me to resume that practice.*

. . . .

*I especially have found comfort in Passover. It was always a time when family would come together and all partake in the readings. I felt closer to my family and God. Today I appreciate how the rituals have existed for centuries, and I find solace in my pain; I'm not alone, others have suffered worse and were freed from their pain. I, too, can be free one day.*

- What principles or characteristics make someone spiritual? Are these characteristics you value, possess, or wish to cultivate?

- Is there someone in your life who you believe possesses these attributes? If so, would you be comfortable talking to them about how they developed these characteristics and maintain them today?

- If faith or religion is not a part of your life, is this something you are or are not open to? Explain your thoughts.

- If you are in a twelve-step program, how would you describe your higher power?

As you practice your faith and experience your spirituality, it helps you:

- Be present in the here and now.
- Find meaning in a higher goal or purpose.
- Stay attuned to your inner guidance.
- Be authentic.
- Monitor your feelings and go inward for answers before relying on others' opinions.
- Put forth the effort.
- Let go of the attachment to the results.

One of the gifts of growing spiritually is that you will learn to trust that life will continue to unfold as it must.

### EXAMPLE

*I practice staying in touch with a loving God on a daily basis. It begins in the morning with a meditation reading from one of those many day-by-day meditation books. My God is a loving, not punishing, God. I believe the love you feel toward others is the essence of God. Accept people for who they are with their imperfections—now that doesn't mean sacrificing myself to a victim role, but that means letting go of judgment of both others and myself and loving myself with healthy boundaries.*

## Wellness Journey

*This section gives you the opportunity to reflect on the movement you have made in your recovery process. It will remind you of why you have been willing to walk through a process that is challenging and certainly, at times, very painful. At the same time, you will recognize the gifts that will continue to come with a commitment to ongoing recovery practice. In your humanness there will be times you may sabotage your recovery and knowing ahead what that sabotage could look like, you can develop an antidote to those moments when it is difficult to keep moving forward. This is your time to develop a concrete plan that will assist your dedication to your recovery process.*

You have done an incredible job getting to this last chapter. To say it hasn't been easy is surely an understatement. Yet, through courage and perseverance, you are developing a foundation that will create an inner strength you have never before experienced. You deserve to feel good about what you've accomplished to this point. You have been willing to go to those dark and painful places within you, to be honest, and to trust in yourself and the process. Certainly you may know you have a long way to go yet, but having tackled the many issues asked of you is truly an accomplishment and reflects a deepening relationship with yourself. As you move forward, we want you to look at the positive changes that have been occurring and to consider those things you will need to continue the momentum in your recovery by defining a personal wellness plan.

Take a moment to acknowledge what you have been doing for yourself, big or small, and write those things down.

**EXAMPLES**

*I used to love knitting and stopped when I was so wrapped up in my marriage. Knitting through the crisis has shown me my creative side and has helped me feel good about me.*

. . . .

*I struggled so much with depression after learning about the addiction. After seeing the weight I put on, I slowly started to exercise. I can't imagine a week now where I don't go for a long walk or meet the trainer at the gym.*

. . . .

*I have been willing to ask questions of my counselor rather than sit in fear.*

. . . .

*I have taken a class on woodworking because I always loved working with my hands.*

. . . .

*I no longer isolate. I am working to identify what is beneath my anger.*

. . . .

*I read daily meditations.*

. . . .

*I have joined a group at my church where am a peer counselor to others. Giving back in this way reminds me of where I was and how my faith has played a big part in my healing.*

- Now take a moment to identify what motivates you to stay on this road of recovery. Write down all that apply to you.

  - To gain self respect.
  - To no longer have to keep lying to myself and others.
  - To find the freedom one experiences from living in truth.
  - To develop skills for maintaining healthy intimacy.
  - To no longer operate from fear.

- To improve my self-esteem.
- To be a better parent and a healthier role model.
- Other.


- To further your motivation, identify and write down those attributes by which you would like to live your life. This may include some of what makes sense to you already, but will also deepen your thoughts to what your recovery could be.

  - Ability to listen to others.
  - Honesty.
  - Prioritize my recovery.
  - Quit putting expectations on recovery.
  - Willingness to try new ideas suggested by those whom I trust.
  - Share both the good and bad in therapy/self-help groups.
  - Learn to trust my voice.
  - Self-love and compassion.
  - Act from a place of self-respect.
  - Other.


To continue in your recovery, key areas to include in your Wellness Plan are:

**Physical**          **Mental**          **Emotional**          **Spiritual**          **Sexual**          **Social**

Each of these areas sustains and nurtures the others. If one is neglected, imbalance and deprivation can set in, spilling over into other areas of your life, interfering with recovery. Going forward means putting your well-being first. Include as many goals as you would like in each of the following six areas. They may be things you want to do differently or goals you have begun to attain and want to sustain.

The following are examples from men and women in recovery.

**Physical**:
*I want to make sure I eat more regularly. I have ignored my body a lot, and paying attention to when I am not hungry is a good way for me to stay in the moment.*

**Mental:**

*I no longer want to spend my days thinking about the addict. I want to focus on my day, my wants and needs.*

**Emotional:**

*I don't want to be so afraid of doing or saying the wrong thing. I want to learn to trust myself more.*

**Spiritual:**

*I no longer want to spend my time trying to control people, places, and things. I want to genuinely grasp that I am truly not in control of everything.*

**Sexual:**

*I want to be more open to exploring my fears around sex and how they are tied to the addiction.*

**Social:**

*I am open to meeting others who have been in similar situations as me.*

Now identify for yourself what goals you would like to achieve within each area.

- Physical
- Mental
- Emotional
- Spiritual
- Sexual
- Social

In this process your energy for sustaining recovery can shift so it is critical to recognize how you might sabotage your progress. Self-sabotaging behaviors are often preceded by self-defeating thoughts and emotions. Based on the ways you are behaving, consider how you might challenge your thinking. For example:

**Thought**: *I tell myself I have nothing in common with the other people at the twelve-step meetings and I stop going.*

**Counter**: *When I hear myself thinking that I am different than others, I will seek out a sponsor.*

**Behavior**: *I am flirting with someone online.*

**Counter**: *I will tell my therapist and commit to being accountable for my time on the computer.*

Write down three self-sabotaging thoughts or behaviors that you think you engage in and then identify counterthoughts or behaviors.

Recovery is about connection with others as much as it is about deepening a relationship with yourself. Your journey need not be done in isolation. Allow others to be a part of your recovery.

Make a list of names and phone numbers for people you know you can count on to reach out to and be available to you during this process. These names may change in time, but always keep at least three people in your inner support circle. Further, consider those in your life who give you joy, satisfaction, and otherwise good feelings about your life. Include them as well and plan how you will reach out to them.

Having a wellness plan contributes to your developing sense of self and makes you better equipped to handle life going forward. Coming to terms with what brought you here and taking the risk to not only overcome it, but face it with a newfound resolve makes you more resilient.

It is important to be able to identify what you are doing that sustains you in recovery. Owning those practices in your recovery means you are more likely to maintain them. The following list identifies useful ways partners sustain their recovery practices.

Identify those practices you are already using and those you wish to incorporate into your wellness plan.

- Journal writing.
- Meditation.
- Therapy.
- Twelve-step work.
- Prayer.
- Exercise/movement therapy.
- Other.

- Now take a moment and consider the outcome of your choices in five years if you stopped working on recovery.

**EXAMPLE**

*If I don't further any recovery or healing practices, five years from now I could anticipate . . . .*

. . . .

*If I further my recovery or healing practice, five years from now I could anticipate . . . .*

Success in recovery is dependent on certain tasks, and committing to a wellness plan means you need to make *you* a priority. Partners have found that what helps them in their ongoing healing is dedicating themselves to their recovery. Not everyone follows the same plan, but one common denominator is a commitment to self-awareness and growth.

# YOUR JOURNEY CONTINUES

To finish a book usually means the story has ended. But with *Intimate Treason*, working your way through to the ending has become a part of a new beginning. Some of you already have been in the process of *reclaiming* yourselves; others are just now *claiming* yourselves for the first time. You have been challenged to experience a depth of honesty that many don't allow themselves, and to take risks that range from terrifying to exhilarating. You have looked at extraordinarily painful issues, but by walking through the pain and owning it, you have found and will continue to find the answers you need that will help you to keep moving forward. We thank you for allowing us to be a part of your journey.

# RESOURCES

## RECOMMENDED READING

*Back from Betrayal*, 2nd Ed., Jennifer P. Schneider, MD, Recovery Resource Press, 2001

*Boundaries and Relationships,* Charlie Whitfield, MD, HCI, 1994

*Boundaries: Where You End and I Begin,* Anne Katherine, MA, MJF Books, 1998

*Codependent No More*, Melody Beattie, Harper/Hazelden, 1986

*Deceived: Facing Sexual Betrayal, Lies and Secrets,* Claudia Black, PhD, Hazelden, 2009

*Disclosing Secrets*, 3rd Ed., Deborah M. Corley, PhD, Jennifer P. Schneider, MD, PhD, Recovery Resource Press, 2004

*Facing Codependence*, Pia Mellody, Andrea W. Miller, Keith Miller, Harper One, 2003

*Facing Love Addiction,* Pia Mellody, Andrea W. Miller, Keith Miller, Harper One, 2003

*Healing the Shame that Binds You*, John Bradshaw, HCI, 1998

*Is It Love or Addiction?*, Brenda Schaefer, Hazelden, 2009

*Love, Infidelity, and Sexual Addiction,* Christine Adams, Authors Choice Press, 2000

*Mending a Shattered Heart*, Stefanie Carnes, PhD, Gentle Path Press, 2008

*Open Hearts*, Patrick Carnes, PhD, Debra Laaser, Mark Laaser, PhD, Gentle Path Press, 1999

*Ready to Heal*, Kelly McDaniel, Gentle Path Press, 2008

*Sex, Lies, and Forgiveness*, Jennifer Schneider, MD, Burt Schneider, Recovery Resource Press, 2004

*Sexual Anorexia*, Patrick Carnes, PhD, Joseph M. Moriarity, Hazelden, 1997

*Shattered Vows*, Debra Laaser, Zondervan, 2008

*Surviving Betrayal*, Alice May, Harper One, 1999

*The Betrayal Bond*, Patrick Carnes, PhD, HCI, 1997

*The Wizard of Oz and Other Narcissists*, Eleanor Payson, Julian Day Publications, 2002

*Women, Sex, and Addiction*, Charlotte Kasl, PhD, Harper Perennial, 1990

## SUPPORT/SELF-HELP/TWELVE-STEP GROUPS

**S-Anon**
800.210.8141
Email: sanon@sanon.org
Website: www.sanon.org

**Co-Sex & Love Addicts Anonymous (COSLAA)**
860.456.0032
Website: www.coslaa.org

**Codependents Anonymous (CODA)**
602.277.7991
706.648.6868
Email: outreach@coda.org
Website: www.codependents.org

## Overcomers Outreach (OO)

800.310.3001

Email: info@overcomersoutreach.org

Website: www.overcomersoutreach.org

## Sexual Recovery Anonymous (SRA)

212.340.4650

Email: info@sexualrecovery.org

Website: www.sexualrecovery.org

## Sex and Love Addicts Anonymous (SLAA)

210.828.7922

Email: info@slaafws.org

Website: www.slaafws.org

## Sexaholics Anonymous (SA)

866.424.8777

Email: saico@sa.org

Website: www.sa.org

## Alcoholics Anonymous (AA)

212.870.3400

Website: www.alcoholics-anonymous.org

## Families Anonymous (FA)

800.736.9805

Email: famanon@familiesanonymous.org

Website: www.familiesanonymous.org

## Co-Sex Addicts Anonymous (COSA)

763.537.6904

Email: info@cosa-recovery.org

Website: www.cosa-recovery.org

## Recovering Couples Anonymous (RCA)

510.663.2312

Email: rca_email@recovering-couples.org

Website: www.recovering-couples.org

**Society for the Advancement of Sexual Health (SASH)**

770.541.9912

Email: sash@sash.net

Website: www.sash.net

**International Institute for Trauma & Addiction Professionals (IITAP)**

866.575.6853

Email: info@iitap.com

Website: www.iitap.com

**Sexual Compulsives Anonymous (SCA)**

800.977.4325

Email: info@sca-recovery.org

Website: www.sca-recovery.org

**Sex Addicts Anonymous (SAA)**

800.477.8191

Email: info@saa-recovery.org

Website: www.sexaa.org

**Adult Children of Alcoholics (ACA)**

310.534.1815

Email: info@adultchildren.org

Website: www.adultchildren.org

**Al-Anon / Al-Ateen**

800.344.2666 Al-Anon

757.563.1600 Al-Ateen

Email: wso@al-anon.org

Website: www.al-anon-alateen.org

# HELPFUL WEBSITES

The following are websites to find therapists trained in specialized treatment modalities.

**Eye Movement Desensitization and Reprocessing (EMDR)**
www.emdr.com/find-a-clinician.html
www.emdria.org

**Somatic Experiencing (SE)**
www.traumahealing.com/somatic-experiencing/practitioner-directory.html

**Sensorimotor Psychotherapy (SPI)**
www.sensorimotorpsychotherapy.org

**Thought Field Therapy (TFT)**
www.tftpractitioners.com

**Emotionally Focused Therapy (EFT)**
www.iceeft.com

**Energy Psychology (EP)**
www.energypsych.org

# ABOUT THE AUTHORS

**Claudia Black, MSW, PhD** is one of the most recognized women in the field of addictive disorders; she is a renowned author and trainer internationally acknowledged for her pioneering and contemporary work with family systems and addictive disorders. She has always brought heart and soul to her work beginning with her seminal work with children of alcoholics and adult children in the late 1970s. She has shared her message of understanding and hope in all corners of the world from Iceland to Australia, Japan to Mexico touching the lives of women and men, young and old. For over thirty years, she has been enthusiastically received as she has trained thousands of addiction specialists and mental health practitioners in issues related to family violence, multi-addictions, relapse, anger, depression, sex addiction, and women's issues.

Dr. Black is Senior Clinical and Family Services Advisor at Las Vegas Recovery Center and Senior Editorial Advisor at Central Recovery Press. She presently serves on the National Association of Children of Alcoholics Advisory Board and on the Advisory Council of the Moyer Foundation, helping children in distress. In 2004, she was the recipient of the Distinguished Alumni Award from the School of Social Work at the University of Washington.

*Intimate Treason* is Claudia's seventeenth book. She has also produced several audio CDs and over twenty DVDs related to addiction issues. For more information on Dr. Black's other materials, her presentation schedule, blog, and newsletter, visit her website at www. claudiablack.com or email info@claudiablack.com.

**Cara Tripodi, LCSW, CSAT** is the Executive Director and owner of STAR (Sexual Trauma & Recovery, Inc.) in Wynnewood, Pennsylvania, specializing in the treatment of sex and love addicts, their partners, and other related traumas. STAR is the largest outpatient treatment program for sex and love addiction in the Philadelphia area. Ms. Tripodi has written about partners of sex addicts in the *Journal of Sexual Addiction & Compulsivity* and in the book, *Mending a Shattered Heart*. She speaks to professional groups locally and nationally on topics pertaining to sexual addiction and is a current board member for the Society for the Advancement of Sexual Health (SASH).

For more information on Ms. Tripodi and STAR, visit her website at www.starhealing.org or call her office 610.658.2737.